UNSTOPPABLE

UNSTOPPABLE

Motivation Secrets You Need to Develop Courage, Confidence, and a Positive Mental Attitude

BRIAN TRACY

MEDIA

Published 2023 by Gildan Media LLC
aka G&D Media
www.GandDmedia.com

Front cover design by David Rheinhardt of Pyrographx

Interior design by Meghan Day Healey of Story Horse, LLC

Library of Congress Cataloging-in-Publication Data is available upon request

ISBN: 978-1-7225-0622-3

10   9   8   7   6   5   4   3   2   1

CONTENTS

FOREWORD   vii

ONE The Power of Motivation   1

TWO The Myths of Motivation   21

THREE Turning On Your Action Mechanism   37

FOUR From Goal Setting to Goal Getting   53

FIVE Right Action and Flexibility   69

SIX The Importance of Daily Self-Talk   87

SEVEN Thinking in the Long Term   103

EIGHT The Keys to Resilience   123

NINE Motivating Others   145

TEN The Power of Rituals   165

FOREWORD

The legendary college football coach Lou Holtz once said, "When all is said and done, more is said than done." These words explain one of the biggest predicaments that we face today. Many of us say we want to be successful, happy, and influential. Yet very few of us follow up with actions that move us toward those goals.

Success is an attractive dream, but the actions required for it are often difficult and lengthy. Happiness is a universal goal, but, again, the actions required to achieve it often require us to delay temporary gratification and avoid quick fixes.

How can we bridge this gap between what we say we want and what we must do to achieve it? We need goal-oriented motivation. It is the fuel that takes us across the long and uncertain bridge to our desired destination. What would it mean for you to learn how to develop this kind of motivation on demand, sustain it through-

---

"When all is said and done, more is said, than done."
—Lou Holtz, College Football Coach

---

out difficult periods, and instill it so completely into your daily life that it makes the very idea of motivation unnecessary?

In this book, you'll learn that the typical ideas of motivation as something that comes and goes, often out of your control, are completely inaccurate. Motivation has been scientifically studied. If you implement these findings, which are described in detail here, you will and must produce the effects that you desire.

Brian Tracy is one of the world's foremost authorities on business and personal success. He has given more than 5,000 talks and seminars to over five million people and is a business coach to top leaders in major industries worldwide.

If you apply Brian's advice to your life, your dreams will become your destiny.

ONE

The Power of Motivation

There's an idea out there that you need talent, brains, and education to be successful in this world, and that these things are sufficient for success.

I started off my life humbly. I didn't graduate from high school, and I worked at laboring jobs. The first job I got was washing dishes in the back of a small hotel. All the time I was growing up, I unfortunately received no motivation aside from threats and punishment from my parents and family. I was told that if you don't get a good education, you won't be successful. If you don't get a good education, you won't go to college; you won't get a good job, you won't marry well, and you'll have to struggle. This is used as a threat to encourage students to do better.

However, what I absorbed is that if I didn't get a good education, I've missed the boat and all I could do was laboring jobs. And that's what I did. I worked at a variety of them, and my only thought was "I didn't graduate from high school, so I'll just seek out more laboring jobs." I worked in sawmills. I worked in the brush with a chain saw. I worked on farms, on ranches. I worked

in factories. I worked in sawmills stacking lumber. I worked digging ditches. All basically Joe jobs, minimum wage jobs, and the
minimum wage was much lower than it is today.

When I could no longer find a laboring job because of the
economy, I got a job making sales, 100 percent on commission,
working from door to door. I worked at that for months.

The Sales Process

Then I had a turning point. I noticed that one guy, who was selling the same product out of the same office, was earning ten times
as much as anyone else, and he wasn't even working very hard. I
was getting up at 6:00 in the morning and preparing. I was out
there knocking on doors when people came to work at 8:00 or
8:30. I'd knock on doors all day long. At night I'd go out and
knock on more doors. I'd maybe make one sale all day.

This guy made four or five sales a day. He'd start at 9:30, quit
at 4:30, and go out to nightclubs. He always had lots of money,
and he was only about three or four years older than me. He was
pretty casual. He didn't seem like a genius. He was just a nice guy.

I asked him, "Why are you so much more successful than I am?"

He said, "Show me your sales process, and I'll critique it for
you."

"I don't have a sales process," I said.

"A sales process is like a recipe. If you don't have one, you're
not going to be successful in preparing a dish."

When I met a prospect, I would talk as fast as I could to get
them interested in my product before they shut down and told
me, "I've got to get back to work. Leave it with me, and I'll look
it over."

"No, no, no," said this salesman. "You have to separate prospects from suspects. You have to ask questions to find out if this person can actually use our product."

He showed me his sales process. It was pretty basic: when you meet a prospect, you just ask questions. I began to ask questions and started to get better results. I went back to this man and asked, "What else can you do?"

"Have you read any books on sales?"

I had no idea there were books on sales. I started to buy and read every book on the subject from cover to cover and underline in them.

Then I heard about audio programs on sales. Those were on cassettes at the time, and I began to listen to audio cassettes every spare minute. Between calls I would listen to a cassette on sales. Then I'd go in to see a person; I'd remember what I learned on the cassette and try it out.

Then I went to my first sales seminar. I learned two things here. Number one is that all success skills are learnable. You can learn any skill you need to learn to achieve any goal you can set for yourself. Before that, I thought that my life was fated for under-achievement, because all I'd ever done was work at laboring jobs and get fired. I slept on the street and in my car. I slept on the floor at friends' apartments. Suddenly I realized that your destiny is in your own hands, that you can learn any skill you need to learn. This motivated me then, and it motivates me now.

"Suddenly I realized that your destiny is in your own hands, that you can learn any skill you need to learn. This motivated me then, and it motivates me now." —Brian Tracy

---

Whenever I see a subject that's of interest to me, I pounce on it. Today, when I go onto Amazon, I find the highest-rated books on the subject. I get them and read them from cover to cover, underlining. Then, because I'm a teacher, speaker, and presenter, I incorporate these ideas into my seminars. My audiences come up to me and say, "I never thought of that before; that is a great idea."

A client in Stockholm came back to me one year after a seminar. He said, "That one idea in your seminar has enabled us to increase our business fifteen times in the last twelve months in a very competitive market. As you recommended, we changed the whole focus of our business to getting more referrals from happy customers. That meant making sure that every customer was extremely happy—so happy they would spontaneously bring their friends. We grew our business fifteen times. We're exploding with that one idea from your seminar. I paid $500 for it, and it's been worth millions to us."

Study after study has been done at Harvard and other universities about natural intelligence, excellent grades, and so on. None of them have any correlation with success. There are people who came to this country with no degrees, no language skills, and no money, and today they're millionaires. There are people who grew up on farms who own their own multinational businesses. There are people who came from the wealthiest homes who are driving taxis. There's no correlation between success and education, skills, family, or even luck. It's all determined by the individual. Every individual has the capability of accomplishing extraordinary things. They just have to learn how to do it.

Your Unlimited Potential

Your initial environment is extremely important, but it does not determine your future. When I was twenty-one years old and struggling, I came across a book on the psychologist Abraham Maslow, which I read from cover to cover. It says that the average individual has extraordinary potential. We don't use 10 percent of our potential, as is commonly said; we use more like 2 percent. As my friend Denis Waitley says, "You have more potential than you could use in a hundred lifetimes."

How do you get that potential out? The self-concept is central here: the way you think about yourself, feel about yourself, see yourself. You will always perform consistently with the person you think you are on the inside. The starting point of all performance change is to change your self-concept.

**"You have more potential than you could use
in a hundred lifetimes."
—Denis Waitley, Best-selling author**

Your self-concept is initially formed by the way your parents treat you. Whenever you see an unhappy or dysfunctional adult, you see a bad childhood. The English poet Alexander Pope wrote, "As a twig is bent, the tree is inclined," which means that if you're bent toward negativity when you're young, you'll become increasingly negative as you get older. More than anything else, the way you think about yourself and your possibilities determines your success.

No matter what your background is, at a certain point, it's your turn to drive. You slip behind the wheel of your own car, and you can decide where you're going to go. You can decide the thoughts that you're going to think, how you're going to think them, and how you're going to interpret things. Nothing from your past can have any influence over you except the influence that you allow it to have.

Psychologist Martin Seligman's work has had a profound effect on my thinking. He found that optimism is the most important predictor of success and happiness. Optimism can be measured in a basic test, and it can be measured again later to determine if you're becoming more and more optimistic.

Here are three questions we sometimes ask at the beginning of my seminars:

1. Complete the sentence "I am." What words come to your mind when you say, "I am"? They describe your self-image and your self-valuation.

   Some people describe themselves by saying, "I am a happy person, a good father or mother, an excellent worker with tremendous and unlimited potential." That's a really good self-concept to have, because it will give you the energy and power to overcome almost any adversity. Other people will say negative things: "I'm an average person. I have nothing but problems and difficulties, and I keep on hanging in there believing that things will get better." Two different world-views—and everybody's got a worldview.

2. I ask participants to describe people. The best ones say, "People are interesting. People are amazing. People are so different. People are fascinating." They'll talk in positive terms. Negative people will say, "People are no good. They're always out to take advantage of you. People are crooks."

3. I ask, "What is life?" Most social problems come from people who think that life is oppressive and unfair and that incomes

are unfairly unequal. Successful people say, "Life is wonderful. It's a great adventure. It beats the alternative. It's getting better and better. It's under your control."

Those worldviews determine the direction your life will go in.

Here's the wonderful thing: at any time in your life, you can choose to change your direction, just as you can wrench the wheel of your car and take a different road. Every major change in a person's life comes when their mind collides with a new idea. Here the new idea is, *you can do anything you put your mind to.*

I was listening to a woman who was worth more than $100 million; she's on *Shark Tank.* She was asked what her philosophy is. She said, "My parents always told me I could do anything in the world, that there was no limit on what I could accomplish. I grew up absolutely believing that, and it turned out to be true."

Of course the people closest to you, especially your family, have the greatest power of suggestion or influence. Then there are your coworkers, your boss, and society as a whole. Even people in your peer group will often try to tear you down when you're trying to be successful or do something extraordinary.

Society often seems to demotivate us. The media work on the premise that bad news and crisis sell: if it bleeds, it leads. There seems to be an aspect of our society that is putting out all the wrong messages, serving to pull people back to the average. People are greatly influenced by their milieus. If you do not have a

---

At any time in your life, you can choose to change your direction, just as you can wrench the wheel of your car and take a different road.

---

clear sense of yourself, a clear center, you can be easily influenced by all the negative things you hear.

I recommend controlling your suggestive environment, which is like the emotional and mental pool you swim in. Rich people watch an average of one hour of television each day, and they carefully select what they watch. Poor people watch five to seven hours, and they watch whatever is on.

If you get down to the bottom line, we are still living in the best time in all of human history. We can live longer. We can live better. We can live healthier. We have more choices. Of course, we have a lot of problems, but one of my great rules is, never worry about things you can't do anything about. You cannot change many of the negative parts of our society. All you can do is change yourself.

Albert Jay Nock, one of the great thinkers of the last century, said, "Each one improve one. Your major business in life is to present society with one improved unit, yourself, and if you make yourself better by that very action, you raise the entire average of your entire society, and that is completely under your control." What a great guiding influence! The more you get better and better, the more, in your own little way, you raise the entire average of the society you live in.

The Power of Responsibility

You have to separate things that are under your control from things that aren't. We cannot control pandemic viruses or acts of terrorism in faraway places. We can't control whether a loved one passes away. The only thing that we can control is ourselves. We can control our own emotions and thoughts.

If you accept responsibility by saying *I am responsible, I am responsible, I am responsible*, you instantly stop all negative emotions.

Say you're in a business crisis. The market goes down. The competition comes up with something that's twice as good and half the price. Even here, there *is* something that under your control: you can accept responsibility.

I've spent thousands of hours studying positive emotions, and I've found that everyone wants to be happy. Why aren't people happy? The block is always negative emotions, a negative self-concept, or a negative idea.

Negative emotions come down to anger, whether they are expressed inwardly or outwardly. These feelings of anger in turn come down to one thing: *blame.* Blame is the essential reason for all negative emotions. If you stop blaming, negative emotions will also stop.

How do you stop blaming? It's very simple. You simply accept responsibility. Your mind can only hold one thought at a time, positive or negative. If you accept responsibility by saying the magic words *I am responsible, I am responsible, I am responsible*, you instantly stop all negative emotions, because you cannot accept responsibility and be negative at the same time.

If you do something over and over again, you develop a habit. Develop a habit of accepting responsibility for any difficulty in your life—of which there will be an endless number—and then take action and do whatever you can. If something happens to someone in your family, ask, "I am responsible; what actions can I take?" Then take those actions.

Because you can only think of one thing at a time, when you take action of any kind, you forget instantly about the negative emotions. You cannot be acting and thinking negatively at the same time. That's why the best cure for worry is continuous action in the direction of your goal. The best way to eliminate any negative feeling is to accept responsibility, and then get busy.

Theodore Roosevelt had a beautiful line: "Do what you can with what you have, right where you are." The only point you can control is this moment. Do what you can with what you have, right where you are. Accept responsibility and take action. Positive emotions will replace the negative emotions, because nature abhors a vacuum. Accepting responsibility is the turning point in taking complete control of your personal development, improving your self-concept, and raising your self-esteem and self-confidence.

If you can get rid of negative emotions, you become a completely positive person. If you repeat the process over and over again, pretty soon you're a happy person all the time. You're not angry with anybody. It doesn't mean that you don't disagree with or disapprove of certain behaviors, but you're not angry about them. People who are in control of their own emotions may disagree, but they're not disagreeable.

Many creative ideas are stillborn. They are never given birth because of a lack of motivation. There are people that have a certain level of creativity and ability, but they never give birth to it. The only thing that separates out the successful ones is the motivation to get it done.

To go back to early childhood experiences, you can grow up with a semiautomatic response to any opportunity. The first response of the person who has had a difficult upbringing—and the most ruinous of all actions that human beings can take—is destructive criticism. Destructive criticism triggers anger and negativity in the recipient. I call it a mental cancer. When this kind of person has an experience or an opportunity, the very first automatic reaction is "Wouldn't that be great!" and the second reaction is "But I can't, I can't because . . ." They trot out all the old reasons: *I don't have enough time. I don't have enough money. I'm not well educated. I'm just too tired at the end of the day.* They go on and on automatically. They stomp out the fire of motivation before it even gets going.

The Comfort Zone

Here are the three major reasons people do not accomplish things. The first is the *comfort zone.* The comfort zone is the greatest enemy of success today. People may fight to get into a comfort zone, or they may get into it gradually or unknowingly, but then they fight like terriers to stay there, even when they know it's not a good place to be.

Apple came out with the iPhone in 2006–2007, and it had incredible features that had never been in a cellular phone before. The senior executives at Nokia and Blackberry, who dominated the cell phone market, looked at it and said, "It's just a fad. It's just for kids." They ignored it. That year, Blackberry cut its research and development budget by 50 percent, because they said, "We don't need to upgrade or improve our phones: we've got 49 percent of the world business market," and they did. Nokia had 50 percent of the world's cellular phone market, and they said, "We don't need to change anything. Everybody loves our products. Why wouldn't they? We're the biggest and the best in the world."

Five years later, both companies were gone because they could not get out of their comfort zone. They didn't realize that the iPhone changed the entire world of communications. They say that the average person with an iPhone has over a billion times the computing power of the first computers put together in 1947. And what you'll be able to do with your cell phone in another five years is beyond our imagination.

The comfort zone is a great killer. Ask yourself, "Am I holding myself back by refusing to accept that the world is changing?" And the world *is* changing. Eighty percent of all products and services that we're using today will be obsolete and gone from the market within five years and will be replaced with brand-new products. Eighty percent of jobs will have changed dramatically.

In America we lose about 3 million jobs a year, and we create another 3.2 million jobs, so there's a huge ebb and flow. Three million jobs are made obsolete by changes in the market, taste, and everything else. Fortunately, because of the dynamism of the American economy, 3.2 million jobs on average are created. Not only are we replacing the jobs that have been made obsolete, but we've added hundreds of thousands more. That's the way our economy normally grows; that's how we maintain low levels of unemployment.

How do you get people out of their comfort zone? Warren Bennis did a best-selling book called *Leaders*. They studied ninety-three leaders over a five-year period. These were top people: university presidents, top corporation presidents, the head of a philharmonic orchestra. The researchers even lived in their homes to watch them and find out how they were different.

One thing was, leaders were always conscious of slipping into a comfort zone. They kept themselves out of the comfort zone by

---

Am I holding myself back by refusing to accept that the world is changing?

---

setting such big goals for themselves that it was impossible for them to achieve them at their current level of activity. They would have to move out of their comfort zone to accomplish these huge goals.

Fear of Failure

The second reason people don't accomplish things is *fear of failure.* Fear of failure is characterized by the words, "I can't. I can't. I'd like to do it, but I can't, because . . ." Successful people turn it around and say, "I can do anything I put my mind to. The only question is how? Where can I learn how? I'll get a book. I'll talk to somebody. I'll go online." It never occurs to them that they can't do something.

Not Knowing How

The third major reason people don't accomplish things is that they feel that they don't know how to make the change. They feel ignorant. *Of course I'd like to start a business, but I don't know how.* I once put together a program called How to Start, Build, Manage, or Turn Around Any Business. It became the best-selling program on startups and business growth in the world. I'm still being asked to give parts of it.

Eighty-two percent of American adults say they want to write a book, but they don't know where to start. I put together a program, *How to Write a Book and Get Published.* People take it, and

---

The 3 Main Reasons People Don't Accomplish What They Want:

1. The Comfort Zone
2. Fear of Failure
3. They Don't Know How

---

they're astonished. Within ninety days they've got a book and a publisher, although they'd been dreaming about it for years.

Those are the three reasons: people become too comfortable; they have natural fears, which come from destructive criticism in childhood and perhaps early failures; and they're ignorant; they don't know how.

Freedom to Choose

We worry about being replaced by computers, but computers are stimulus-response: they get an input and respond in a certain way. Animals are very much the same way: basically, there is a stimulus, and then there is a response.

Human beings are different. They encounter a stimulus, then there's a response, but in the middle there's a freedom to choose. There's a moment where you can think. As your mother told you, stop and think before you act. Stop and think before you speak. Rich people stop and think before they speak. Poor people say whatever is on their mind. You don't have to say everything you're thinking. You don't have to blurt anything out, so just stop.

I've found that if you're on the verge of saying something and the other person interrupts you, it's God's way of telling you not to speak. Instead of trying to speak over the other person or win the discussion, stop and think. People cause problems by saying things without giving them enough thought. In fact, that's a major reason for failure.

Successful people stop and think, sometimes for a long time. Management guru Peter Drucker said, "Fast people decisions are invariably wrong people decisions." He said, "Whenever you have to make a decision with futurity"—which means it's going to last for a long time—"take a lot of time to think. Take a day; take a weekend."

An excellent book was recently written about decision making. The writer's major point was this: the more time you can put between the stimulus and the response, the more effective the response will be, and the better the decision will be. That's why people often advise, "Sleep on it." If you have to make any kind of a decision that has futurity, say, "Let me think about it for a couple of days." If somebody wants to borrow money or sell you something, say, "It sounds like a good idea, but let me think about it for a while."

The biggest mistakes I've ever made happened when I responded too quickly without giving it any thought. Later I said, "I could kick myself. Why didn't I just take some time to think about that? Why did I respond in such a knee-jerk way?"

Many years ago, I had a mentor who had a great effect on me. He gave me a beautiful old book from the 1920s called *Take Time Out for Mental Digestion*. It explains how you need seventy-two hours to incorporate a new idea into your thinking. When you

---

"Fast people decisions are invariably wrong people decisions."
—Peter Drucker, Management Guru

---

have a new idea or opportunity, always take seventy-two hours to think about it and turn it over in your mind. Look at it from several different aspects before you decide.

Working as a personal advisor to extremely wealthy people, I've found that they take a lot of time to make decisions. They do a lot of research. They do a lot of pondering. They talk it over with other intelligent people. They ask for more information. As a result, when they do make the decision, it is vastly better than if they had reacted immediately.

Successful people tend to be more thoughtful than unsuccessful people. It's not that they're smarter; they just take more time and gather more information. They use that middle point between stimulus and response. They use that moment very carefully. They're free to choose the time of the response.

Drucker used to say that if you're going to hire someone, take a week, take a month, spend some time with them, but go very slowly, especially if you're starting a business or running a fast-growing business. Be very careful, because if you hire the wrong person, the complexities and costs can be tremendous, especially for a small business. Every businessperson has thought, "If I had given it a little more thought, I would have never hired him or her in the first place."

That's how you work. You take the time, sit down, turn off the computer and phone, sit quietly, and think about important decisions. This is one of the greatest discoveries for success.

Doubling Your Income

One question I ask my audiences is, "How many people here would like to double their income?" Of course everybody raises their hand. I say, "That's good, because you are going to double your income. As an economist I can guarantee that everyone here in this room is going to double their income if they live long enough, because if your income goes up at an average of about 3 percent per annum using compound interest, you'll double your income in twenty-two years. Is that what you have in mind?"

Everybody says, "No, no."

So you want to double your income much faster. All right. Here's an interesting discovery. If you increase your income by 25 percent per year, with compounding, you'll double your income in three years. If you continue to increase your income at 25 percent per year for ten years, you'll increase your income ten times.

How do you increase your income 25 percent per year? You increase it 2 percent per month, or 0.5 percent a week. If you become more productive by 0.05 percent each week, 2 percent a month, the compounding effect will guarantee that you'll double and double again. You'll become one of the highest-paid people in society, completely irrespective of your background, grades, friends, contacts, or the state of the economy. Just take the first step.

Time management is very simple: plan every day in advance. Decide on your most important task. Start on that task first, and complete it before you go on to number two. I've written a book on this; it is the best-selling book on time management in history, with 6 million copies sold in forty-two languages. It teaches every single part of time management, but it distills it down to this: choose your most important task. Start on that first thing, and stay with it until it's done. If you do that, you'll double your productivity next week, and your income will soon catch up with your productivity.

You succeed one step at a time. You don't have to transform your life. As you begin to apply these techniques, you'll see results within a week.

Results motivate people. Daniel Pink wrote a book called *Drive: The Surprising Truth about What Motivates Us*, which was a state-of-the-art analysis of what drives people. The answer was forward motion, progress, the feeling *I'm getting better in my job. I'm making progress in my career. I am earning more money. I'm achieving more of my goals. I'm doing more of the things that I want to do.* This feeling of forward movement is the greatest motivator of all, and it's totally under the individual's control.

Motivation Requires a Motive

Motivation requires a motive. Often people are not motivated because they have no motive. They have no *why*. They have no goal. They have nothing great that they want to accomplish.

If they come across something that really excites them, suddenly they're motivated. They're up out of bed early in the morning. They're into their work all day long. They're busy in the evening. They become impatient with small talk, because now they've got a motive; they've got something big that they want to accomplish.

Each person is responsible for determining their motive, their *why*, what they want to accomplish. One best-selling book, *Start with Why* by Simon Sinek, suggests that you ask, why are you doing what you're doing? Why do you get up in the morning? What are your values? You may say, "I want to earn more money so that I can create a better life for my family and can create opportunities for my children." That's what will get you out of bed in the morning.

Essentials of Time Management
To Double Your Productivity:

- Plan every day in advance.
- Decide on your most important task.
- Start on that task first, and complete it entirely before going on to your next task.
- Succeed one step at a time.

TWO

The Myths of Motivation

I believe there are two types of motivation: *false motivation* and *true motivation*. False motivation is telling you stories about how you can do anything. Some very successful people teach this. It's a feel-good type of motivation, like going to a movie or a rock concert, but it has no lasting value. People forget 80 or 90 percent of what they heard, even though they felt good when they were listening to it.

True motivation, in my estimation, comes from an enhanced feeling of competence. The speaker gives you specific ways to achieve your goals faster and have a better life. That's what motivates people, because when they learn new skills or ideas, they say, "I can do that. That's not complicated. That's very practical, and I can see the results I can get."

People are not motivated unless they can create an exciting visual picture for themselves and think, "I can do that. I can get up a little bit earlier."

Rich people get up before 6 a.m. Poor people get up at 7 a.m. or later. Change your habits, including when you rise. One mentor

---

Two types of motivation:
False motivation: Feel-good type motivation where you tell
yourself "I can do anything."
True motivation: An enhanced feeling of competence from
learning new skills or ideas.

---

of mine made a habit of getting up before 6 a.m. every morning. His company had fifty-two branches and 10,000 employees. He'd started off working at the lowest-level job, in the mail room, and worked himself up. He said to me, "I always get up before 6 a.m. If I go to bed late, I still force myself to get up before 6 a.m. That teaches me not to go to bed late the second night in a row."

If you set a simple discipline about getting up in the morning, the rest of your life iterates almost like an Excel program. It changes everything that happens for the rest of the day.

Your motivation comes from inside yourself, and you can create that motivation. The way you do that is by having something to get yourself out of bed for in the morning.

Your Self-Concept

Motivation has to do with self-concept. In the individual's early formative experiences, were they encouraged, praised, and approved of, and made to feel valuable, important, and smart? In that case, they're going to grow up to be highly motivated and positive about themselves.

Your self-concept is made up of three parts. The first is your *self-ideal*: the person you would ideally like to be. It's your fantasy person—in terms of health, wealth, position, influence, marriage, and everything else. This ideal is either clear, as it is in the minds of successful people, or unclear. Unsuccessful people are vague and unclear about where they would like to be in the future.

If you could wave a magic wand and make your life perfect three years from now, what would it look like, and how would it be different from today? Write it down: How much would you be earning? What kind of home would you live in? What kind of relationships would you have? What level of health and fitness would you have? How much money would you have in the bank?

As people become clear about those things, motivation takes place automatically. So the second part of a self-concept is your *self-image*. The self-image is how you see yourself, and it regulates your performance on a moment to moment basis. We always perform on the outside consistently with the picture we have on the inside. There's a saying, *the person you see is the person you'll be.*

Your self-image is made up of three parts: the way you see yourself, the way others see you, and the way you think others see you. If you think other people see you as an excellent person, you'll be happy when you associate with them. You'll talk and laugh spontaneously, because they're reinforcing your self-image as a likable, attractive, and intelligent person. Similarly, if we think people see us in a negative way, it'll affect our performance in the other direction.

There may be a gap between your *self-image*, the way you see yourself now, and your *self-ideal*, the way you would like to be, and this gap determines your personality. If there's too much of a gap between where you are now and where you feel you should be, it demotivates you. You lose heart.

People say, "I want to be a millionaire." OK, let's write it down, make a plan, set a schedule. "I want to be a millionaire within a year." How much money do you have now? "I'm broke." What sort of work do you do? "I'm unemployed." How much money do you have? "None, I'm deeply in debt."

In this case, setting a goal to be a millionaire, the ideal, contrasted with where you are today, will simply demotivate you. It will not inspire you. You'll take a couple of stabs at it, give up, and tell yourself that it wasn't meant to be anyway.

The third factor is *self-esteem*. Self-esteem is best defined as how much you like, love, value, and appreciate yourself as an important and worthwhile person. This is the reactor core; this is the heartbeat, the critical determinant of your personality. It determines your self-image. As you move from your image of where you are toward your ideal of where you want to be, your self-esteem goes up. You like yourself more, you feel good about yourself, and you feel happy and exuberant.

Ultimately, success is not about material rewards, but about inner joy. You can raise your self-esteem by simply repeating, *I like myself. I like myself. I like myself.*

Once I received a video from a young guy who's extraordinarily successful. For seven minutes, he fired into the video about how bad his life had been. He was selling cellular telephones in a shopping center. He would talk to fifty people, and they'd all tell him to go away. He was in despair. Then he bought and read my book *The Psychology of Selling*, which says that how you feel on the inside determines your success on the outside.

When he went to work the next day, he sat in the car and said, "I like myself. I like myself. I like myself." People were looking at him because he was talking to himself. He went into the shopping center. One potential customer said no, but he said, "Wait a minute. This is really a good choice. This can revolutionize your life."

The three parts of the self-concept

1. Your *self-ideal*: The person you would really like to be.
2. Your *self-image*: The way you see yourself, the way others see you, the way you think others see you.
3. Your *self-esteem*: How much you like, love, value and appreciate yourself.

The young man was on fire, because he had cranked up his self-esteem and self-confidence. The person said, "Really? Tell me more about it," and the young man made his first sale after several days. Then he made his second sale, and his third. Pretty soon he was breaking sales records. He became a supervisor, and then a manager. Then he was hired by a bigger company. He said, "Saying 'I like myself, I like myself, I like myself' transformed my life completely."

The Two Main Pillars

The two most powerful pillars of the mental temple are *I like myself* and *I am responsible*. The more you like yourself, the more responsibility you accept. The more responsibility you accept, the more powerful you feel, and the more you like yourself. There's a direct relationship between how much you like yourself and how positive you are. There's also a direct relationship between how much responsibility you accept, how much you feel in control of your own life, and how happy you are overall. Each one reinforces the other.

Don't go out and *have* a good day; go out and *make it* a good day. We have more opportunities surrounding us today, because there are more products and services being invented and more customer wants and needs that are unsatisfied. Consequently, somebody can always do something to take advantage of the current market situation. But it requires ambition, hard work, persistence, tenacity, and bouncing back over and over. Recent psychological studies say that it all comes down to grit. A person who has grit, determination, and tenacity will not be stopped.

Mike Todd was a great impresario in New York. At one point, he was married to Elizabeth Taylor. He put up the money to sponsor plays. Sometimes they worked; sometimes they didn't. One day he put all of his money behind a play and lost it all, and the announcement was "Mike Todd is broke."

A reporter came and asked, "Mr. Todd, what is it like to be poor?"

He said, "Excuse me, young man, I'm not poor; I'm only broke. Poor is a state of mind; broke is a temporary condition, and I will be back."

And he was. His next show was a great success, and he was back being a multimillionaire and a member of high society.

Broke is a temporary condition; *poor* is a state of mind. If you're poor, you only think of how you can get money from other people. Free money destroys the soul of the recipient. Earned money, earned success, is the foundation principle for self-esteem, self-reliance, self-responsibility, happiness, joy, and energy. When you earn your success, you feel great.

Some say that rich people aren't happy. I've studied the rich, and I can tell you that the rich are very happy, because they have started with nothing. Ninety percent of all successful Americans started with nothing, and they have achieved something worthwhile through years of hard work.

People say these people were just lucky. Then you look at their backgrounds. They started off like me, washing dishes or working on a ship just to get to this country. They lived in slums for years while they were working their way up.

The late Andrew Grove was the president of Intel. He was one of the great entrepreneurs in American history. His name was originally András Gróf, and he was from Hungary. When the Russians overran Hungary in 1956, he fled to New York. He learned English, went to school, and got an engineering degree. Then he went out west, got a business degree, and started at the bottom of a business in San Francisco. Before it was over, he was the president of Intel, the biggest computer chip manufacturer in the world. If you ever listen to him or read anything he wrote, you will see that he was a great man. He arrived here with nothing, a sixteen-year-old fleeing a revolution. People say, "He sure was lucky." But behind every lucky person, there's a long history of hard work and countless failures.

Recently I was talking to somebody who was saying that successful people are just lucky; they just stumbled into it.

I said to him, "You're an intelligent guy. Did you know that successful people fail five and ten times more often than failures do?"

He blew up at me. He said, "That's not true. Successful people just fell into the jam. They stumbled into something, and it turned out to be the right thing."

"No," I said. "Statistically, successful people fail vastly more often than the average person."

Just prior to the break in a radio interview, four self-made millionaires were asked, "How many different businesses have you been in before you got into the one where you made a million dollars?" During the break, they calculated it out. They came back: it was an average of seventeen businesses. They had failed, or semi-failed, in sixteen businesses. It was the seventeenth one, on average, that made them rich.

The millionaires were asked, "Did you actually fail in the first sixteen businesses?" All four of them said, "No, those were the most important learning experiences. Without those failures, we would have never been successful in the business we're in today."

Motivation: Positive and Negative

Myth number three is that motivation can only arise out of positive circumstances. Certainly it helps to be surrounded by a supportive community and have positive inputs. But as we've seen with Andrew Grove, who started out fleeing the Hungarian Revolution, motivation can arise from both positive and negative circumstances.

It's a basic principle in psychology that as adults, we strive to achieve what we felt we were most deprived of as children. If we were deprived of money, we'll aspire to get money. If we were deprived of love, we will strive to get that. If we felt ignored or useless in school, we'll strive for respect from other people.

Most Hollywood actors are driven by this need. When they were young, they were made to feel unimportant and useless. They got the taste of show biz, where people applaud and smile and tell them what a great job they're doing. It becomes a drug.

Henry Ford once said that power is the ultimate aphrodisiac. When you have power, people come to you, shake your hand, ask for your autograph, and listen when you speak. That's moving away from the negative, and it's very common.

I once asked three wealthy businesspeople, "When did you get your first job?" At the age of ten or eleven, they said. When I was ten, my parents told me, "We don't have the money to buy you clothes for school, so you're going to have to earn it yourself." This was in the summertime. I got a garden hoe and went out knocking on doors, asking people if they had any weeds to hoe. One woman had a whole backyard that was overgrown. She said, "Can you hoe those weeds?"

"Absolutely."

"How much do you charge?"

"Twenty-five cents an hour."

"OK," she said.

And I hoed those weeds. I think it took me two weeks to hoe down that whole yard, rake up all that grass, and drag it away. That was my money to buy my clothes for the fall. From that day onward, I never took a penny from my parents. I got up and delivered newspapers at 4:00 and 5:00 a.m.

At the age of fourteen, Warren Buffett didn't have much money. He got up at 4:00 every morning to deliver newspapers. He got one cent of profit for every paper he delivered, and he saved the money, because his parents were paying for his food. He delivered 200,000 newspapers over a period of three or four years. He saved $2,000. That was the starting point for his investments.

Buffett invested $2,000 in 1962. Today he's worth $104 billion. He started with that one penny from delivering each newspaper and saved carefully. People say he's lucky. Yes, and look where he started. That's moving away from the negative.

The positive angle is equally motivational. It's when it occurs to people that they can be vastly more than they are. This is part of Maslow's influence on me when I read his first book. It said you have enormous potential. So while everybody was out socializing and going to bars, I began spending thousands of hours studying. I'd sit at home hour after hour, reading about success. That's when I learned the importance of eliminating negative emotions. If you do, they're automatically replaced by positive emotions, and one form of positive emotion is goals. You start to think about goals.

Ask yourself this question: *what do you really want to do with your life?* Pause, and ask it again: *what do you really, really want to do with your life?* Then pause and ask it one more time: *what do you really, really, really want to do with your life?*

Ask yourself:
What do you really, really, really want to do with your life?

If you had no restrictions, if you could accomplish anything in the world, if you had all the knowledge and ability that you would ever need, what would you do with your life? If you can determine that clearly and can see a picture of what it would look like, you're automatically motivated. It lights up the afterburners in your psyche. You wake up in the morning, and you're wired to move toward that goal.

But you've got to see it clearly. You have to know exactly what you want—what you would want to accomplish if you had no limitations at all. That's what motivates you in a positive way.

The Permanence of Motivation

Myth number four is a subtler one. It says that motivation is a condition of the mind that, once achieved, remains with you for a lifetime. One motivational speaker said, "Once the lights were turned on for me, they've never turned off."

That's what a lot of people hope for. But often motivation must be renewed or restored on a daily basis. If you don't continually renew and restore yourself, even success can start to feel mundane.

Lloyd Conant was a great man, co-founder of Nightingale-Conant Corporation, which produced inspirational recordings. He once told me that you have a template for success in your subconscious mind. It's almost like a framework which fills in, like concrete. Every successful person has achieved one great goal, and as a result, they have a template for success. Nothing will satisfy them more than the achievement of another goal that's even bigger, so all success begins with achieving one big goal.

If you take the well-known 80/20 rule, you'll find that the 20 percent of people who earn 80 percent of the money have, sometime in their lives, started and completed a major goal. It may be as simple as graduating from a university or winning a race. It may be climbing a mountain; it may be writing a book or poem; it may be becoming the president of a society, but they've accomplished something they had to work hard for. It's called *learned success* or *earned achievement*. The resulting joy releases endorphins. Fireworks go off in their brain. Sometimes they'll

---

Earned success is the foundational principle for self-esteem, self-reliance, self-responsibility, happiness, joy and energy.

---

look back decades later and say, "That was the great moment of my life."

From then on, you're programmed, almost like a computer, to achieve another success that's even greater. You'll wake up every morning thinking of your next success. You're looking forward. You read and go to seminars and workshops. You're constantly learning new things in search of your next big success.

Pick one goal that's really important to you. Then put your whole heart into achieving it, no matter how long it takes. Once you do that, you'll become a different person, and a better person, for the rest of your life.

Pick a goal that's really important to you. Then, put your whole heart into achieving it, no matter how long it takes.

Visualization

The way you visualize your success is extremely important.

Once researchers did a study of two teams that played in the Super Bowl. Both teams, of course, had won their leagues and won their divisions. One team beat the other 45–8 or something like that—one of those upset victories.

Researchers interviewed the players on the teams afterwards. Throughout the season, one team had visualized winning every game and running onto the field at the Super Bowl, with hundreds of thousands of people cheering. They visualized this in their locker room, and they talked about it over and over.

The other team was visualizing running *off* the field in the Super Bowl with the trophy. So the one team may have accomplished their goal when they ran onto the field. That was it; they fell apart on the field because they had no further vision. The other team visualized themselves winning this game and running off as champions.

Every goal should lead to a higher goal, and you should already have determined your next goal when you move toward completion of this one, so each goal motivates you even further, like ranges beyond ranges of mountains. Each time you cross a mountain, you see higher and higher mountains.

Motivation Alone Isn't Enough

Myth number five is that motivation alone is sufficient to achieve your goal. The first mistake is thinking, *because I want to, I can*. A lot of people are misled by motivational speakers and books.

A perfect example would be *The Secret* by Rhonda Byrne. It taught that if you could think happy thoughts and visualize happy pictures, all good things would come to you, but nowhere in the book does the word *work* appear. People love the book because they love the idea of being successful without having to work, and it became a best seller.

The idea was if I want to, I can; I just have to have an intense, burning desire. No: that is just the start. After looking at the map and determining your destination, you need to move toward it.

The second thinking error is, *because I have to, I can*. I've *got* to earn this money. I've *got* achieve this goal. But what you *have to* do has no relationship to what you *can* do. One of my favorite lines is, "Pray and then move your feet." It means be really clear about your goal, write it down, and then act.

Any big goal has to be broken down into steps—perhaps twenty, thirty, or forty. Then you take one step at a time. It's like climbing a long staircase: you just plod one step at a time. Each day you get up and work on each of those steps in sequence.

At the beginning, there's very little motivation, because progress seems to be very slow, but there's a law called *the law of accelerating acceleration.* As you move towards your goal, you create a force field in the universe that attracts your goal toward you. Imagine the roundness of the globe. You start to move towards your goal way over on the other side of the globe. The goal starts to move toward you too, but you can't see it, because it's out of sight. Like attracts like; bodies in motion will attract each other. As they move toward each other, they'll start to move faster and faster.

Here's a discovery: 80 percent of your goal will be achieved in the last 20 percent of the time in which you work on it. Many people work for a long time and don't see a lot of progress, yet they hang in there, and then suddenly everything starts to work for them. They move faster and faster, and they achieve the goal, always in a way that's different from what they'd initially expected. The thing is to start by taking one step at a time.

Inspirational speaker Earl Nightingale used to say that happiness is the progressive realization of a worthy ideal or goal. Moving step-by-step towards something that's important to you gives you a continuous feedback of motivation, a continuous source of energy. This mere act of forward motion makes you smarter and more creative.

A principle that comes from Sir Isaac Newton is called *inertia*: a body in motion tends to remain in motion unless acted upon by an outside force. By the outside force, he meant something like gravity: if you threw a ball, the ball would go through the air, then gravity would start to pull it down to the earth. But if the ball was

---

**Eighty percent of your goal will be achieved in the
last twenty percent of the time that you work on it.**

---

in open space, where there is no gravity, you could throw it, and it
would keep moving to infinity.

The Momentum Principle

There is also *the momentum principle of success*: when you start moving toward your goal, progress will seem very slow at the beginning.
This is where most people quit. That's why they say if you want to
lose a lot of weight, don't weigh yourself for the first two weeks of
your regimen, because you won't see any progress, even though
it's taking place below the surface. So wait two weeks; then you
may find you have dropped five pounds. Then you start to become
more confident: *This is working. I can do this. This is worthwhile.* then
somebody asks, "Have you lost weight?" That's considered to be
the best single compliment in America, by the way.

As you move toward your goal, motivation increases. Almost
everything depends upon your belief. If you are certain that you're
going to achieve this goal sooner or later, nothing will stop you.
Each time you take a step toward the goal, your belief grows. It
grows from zero belief or even negative belief.

You can start off with disbelief. You say, *I want to become wealthy,*
but you don't believe it. But you say, *I can become wealthy by setting
goals. I'm going to start to work every day.* As you keep taking steps,
the disbelief begins to dwindle until you reach a psychologically
neutral point: you neither believe nor disbelieve. If you keep on,
you start to believe a little bit more. You keep doing more things,

and your belief starts to grow and grow. Pretty soon you get to the point where your belief is so big that you become unstoppable. Nothing can stop you from your goal, because you absolutely, 100 percent, believe that it's attainable for you, and that becomes true.

Og Mandino, author of *The Greatest Salesman in the World,* once told me, "Brian, there are no secrets of success. There are merely timeless truths that have been learned and repeated over and over again throughout the centuries." The greatest thinkers in antiquity, like Cicero and Plutarch, teach the same principles. You decide very clearly on your objective. Plan your attack, put your plan into action, act immediately, and keep working until you achieve it. It's not a secret. It's been proven over and over by millions of people who are successful today.

Each person has a success mechanism and a failure mechanism. The failure mechanism goes off automatically, which is why 80 percent of the population is mediocre, stuck in the middle, and worried about money all the time.

The success mechanism has to be triggered, and it's triggered by a goal. If you set a goal, the success mechanism becomes the default and shuts off the failure mechanism. You shut off your failure mechanism by overriding it with a goal. As long as you're working on the goal, the failure mechanism never comes on again.

"There are no secrets of success. There are merely timeless truths that have been repeated over and over again throughout the centuries." —Og Mandino, Best-selling author

---

THREE

Turning On Your Action Mechanism

Your self-concept is the master program of your mental computer. Everything you do is a result of what's been programmed into your subconscious Your beliefs are the primary drivers of motivation, because, as the author Anaïs Nin once said, "You do not believe what you see; you see what you already believe."

You go through the world looking through a screen of beliefs, like a lattice that holds up flowers. This screen of beliefs enables you to see some things and keeps you from seeing other things. It causes you to be blinkered, like a horse. You have a narrow view of things, and you can't see anything outside these beliefs.

All beliefs are learned. Your beliefs about yourself, which determine everything you think, feel, or do, are learned from early childhood. Some people are taught positive beliefs. Some people are taught negative beliefs.

Many people all over the world have strong beliefs about their religions. Some are fanatically obsessed with them. But when those people were born, they knew nothing about their religion.

Everything they know, think, believe, even will die for today was taught to them over the years, sometimes accidentally, sometimes deliberately. A belief can be accidentally picked up by reading your horoscope or by having someone tell you something. Unfortunately, many people have beliefs that are simply not true.

Because your beliefs determine everything, the starting point of changing your life is to change your beliefs. Many years ago, I got bronchitis in the middle of December. Bronchitis tires you out. I was a bachelor, and I sat around resting. Because it was around Christmastime, I wasn't working, and it went away.

Around Christmastime the next year, I got bronchitis again; again I had to sit and baby myself for a week. I was convinced that if you have it once, you have it at the same time every year.

Talking to a friend of mine who was a nurse, I said, "I have bronchitis every year around Christmastime."

"That's absolute nonsense," she said.

"Somebody told me that if you have it, you'll have it every year at the same time. It's programmed into your genes."

"That's absolute nonsense. There's no medical foundation for that at all."

"Really?"

"Absolutely."

Ever since then, I have never had bronchitis. This was a false belief, but it was so strong that every year in the middle of December, I would start to have bronchitis. I'd make myself sick with a negative belief.

Because your beliefs determine everything, the starting point of changing your life is to change your beliefs.

Self-Limiting Beliefs

The most hindering beliefs are self-limiting beliefs: You're limited in intelligence, because you didn't get great grades. You're limited in ability, because you did not perform at an excellent level. You're limited in creativity, because you haven't come up with any good ideas. You're limited in athletic ability, artistic ability, and so on. One casual negative remark from someone who you think knows what they're talking about can set you off-course for life. It can come from a casual remark from one of your parents.

My father said, "Brian is completely tone-deaf. He has no ability to listen to or appreciate music." I wanted to get a guitar and play, but he told me I was tone-deaf, and I believed him for years. Then suddenly I realized, "I may not be a Carnegie Hall musician, but I'm not tone-deaf. I enjoy music."

Let me give you a positive example. When my son David was growing up, he would try things, and he would be unsuccessful, as kids are. He would say, "Dad, I don't think I can do this. I'm afraid to fail."

"David, I'm your father," I said, "and I know something about you. I know that you're not afraid of anything."

"Oh, yes. I'm afraid of a lot of things, at sports and school."

"No, you're not. You may think you are, but I'm your father, and I know better. I know that you're not afraid of anything."

I made a game of it. My wife, Barbara, and I would be driving, and David would be in the back seat. I would say, "You know, Barbara, there's one thing I'm really happy about: our son David is not afraid of anything." I would repeat that, and I called him Dave the Brave. I would say, "How's Dave the Brave today?" And I called him Le Brave, Dave Le Brave, in French.

I kept repeating this idea. Then one day, when he was ten or eleven years old, I heard him say to one of his friends, "I know one thing about myself: I'm not afraid of anything."

"It worked," I thought. "I programmed him with positive single messages."

Today David is in residential real estate. He learned how to sell by knocking on doors. He is not afraid of anything.

Challenge Self-Limiting Beliefs

The starting point is to challenge your self-limiting beliefs and ask yourself, "In what area do I feel limited?" I started off with no education, no money, no schooling, so I had a lot of self-limiting beliefs. Then I began to think that they weren't true. It was a real shock. Somebody will tell you something that you believed all your life. When you find that it's not true, it's an amazing revelation.

One guy grew up in a working-class family. His father was a factory worker, and he repeated at the dinner table over and over, "The Wilsons have always been working people, generation after generation. We've always been laborers. We'll always be laborers. When you kids grow up, you'll be laborers as well."

When the guy left school, he got a laboring job. About a year or two later, he was digging a ditch next to the highway, and the traffic had slowed down. A car came along, and there was one of the guys from his high school, who was no smarter or better than

---

Start to challenge your self-limiting beliefs by asking:
In what area do I feel limited?

---

he was but was driving a nice car. He was well dressed. He said, "Glen, how are you doing?"

Glen said, "I'm doing great. I got into sales. I got into life insurance. I'm making great money, just bought a new house. I'm getting married in a year."

The traffic moved on, and away Glen went. The first guy sat there and realized that he had bought his father's beliefs that he was only suited to be a laborer. Then he saw somebody who was no smarter or better than him, but who had a great life.

He got up, threw the shovel in the ditch, and quit. He got a job in sales, and six years later, he was a millionaire with his own business. He remembered that turning point when he realized, "I have been sold a false belief that I'm going to be a laborer all my life."

We all have false beliefs that hold us back. They act like brakes on our potential. A good friend of mine, who's a psychologist and a teacher, wrote a book called *Release Your Brakes*. What are the brakes that are holding you back?

How would you like to earn five times or ten times as much? You're capable of it. How do we know? Because there are lots of people selling the same product in the same market but who are earning five and ten times as much as you. They're no smarter than you; some of them are dumber and less educated than you. (Nothing will make you angrier than to find somebody who's dumber but who's earning more money than you.)

The Principle of Reversibility

It isn't bragging if you've done it, so one way to overcome negative beliefs is to think about the opposite. You say, "I can't earn much more money than I'm earning today. I'm always in debt." Instead say, "I can earn all the money that I want simply by continually upgrading my skills and applying myself diligently, using my time well, and working hard. I can earn the same kind of money that other people do doing the same things."

Then you act. The Bible says that faith without actions is dead. You use the principle of reversibility: if you act as if you already believe that you are meant to be a big success, then you will start to feel and believe it. The action will create the feeling, just as the feeling creates the action.

William James, the founder of American psychology, said that if you want to be self-confident, act as if you already are self-confident—the action will create the emotion. This is how to eliminate self-limiting beliefs: challenge them, and do the opposite.

What if I had all the self-confidence in the world? What if I were not afraid of anything? How would I behave? I would get up early in the morning and go out and knock on every door and ring every telephone, visit every customer, as if I were in a desperate race to see as many people as possible. If you do that, surprise, surprise—you develop the same level of confidence as a person who is already extraordinarily successful.

Mental Laws

There is a series of mental laws. The first is *the law of cause and effect*. It says that for every effect, there is a cause or causes. If you duplicate them, you achieve the same effect.

If you want to double your income, ask what people who are earning twice as much as you are doing that's different from what you're doing. Whatever they tell you, do it without question.

I took karate for ten years and got a black belt in two different fields. In karate, when you start off, you do exactly what you're told to do. You do it hundreds and thousands of times. In that first half of every karate class, you go back and repeat the basics—punching, kicking, moving sideways, forward, backwards. You do that for the first half of the class. In the second half, you do more advanced things, like free fighting. You do it all over and over again. You do everything thousands of times. When you get into competition, your responses are automatic. You don't have to think to act.

It's the same thing if you want to become an athlete. You do exactly what the coach tells you. If you want to become a musician, you do what the music teachers tell you. If you want to do anything, you do the cause, and the effect will follow.

Say your desired effect is to double your income. What are the causes of earning twice as much? Because of the law of cause and effect, if you do what successful people do, you will get the same results they do. There's no mystery.

The second principle is *the law of belief*: whatever you believe with feeling, with conviction, becomes your reality. The intensity of your beliefs creates the reality.

Four Areas of Expectations

The third law is *the law of expectations*. It says that whatever you expect with confidence becomes your own self-fulfilling prophecy.

There are four areas of expectations. The expectations of your parents build happy, healthy, self-confident kids who grow up and become winners in life. One major factor is a democratic environment: the child's opinions are respected and solicited. The child grows up believing that their opinions are valuable, because

> ## The 4 Areas of Expectations
> 1. The expectations of your parents
> 2. The expectations of your boss.
> 3. The expectations of people who look up to you.
> 4. The expectations you have of yourself.

everybody in their family, including these two giants, the parents, have supported them 100 percent.

The second area is the expectations of your boss. Bosses with high expectations build peak performance environments. The boss expects people to do well and believes they can.

The third area is your expectations of the people who look up to you. Your children, spouse, friends, and employees will always rise to your level of expectations. If you have high expectations for them, they will not disappoint you.

The fourth area is your expectations of yourself. You can never be greater or more successful on the outside than you expect to be on the inside.

Imagine you could buy an operating program that you could slide into your brain, which would operate on it for the rest of your life. What would be the best program to buy? Buy the one that says that you are going to be a great success. Program that into your brain so that no matter what happens, you expect to succeed, to learn, to benefit, to prosper.

Many people lose their fortunes, even billions of dollars. Two or three years later, they're back. What happened? Their belief was solid. Their mental set was more powerful than all the facts in the world.

Your expectations determine your actions. Your expectations determine your attitude. Earl Nightingale said that *attitude* is the most important word in the language.

Your attitude toward other people—is it positive; are you cheerful? Are you warm, genial, friendly? Do you have high energy? If you expect to be successful, to be liked, and to learn something from every setback, your attitude is going to be positive, which is the foundation for success.

Your attitude starts with your *values*: what you believe is important. It then spreads to your *beliefs*, because your values determine your beliefs about reality, which then go out in concentric circles.

The next circle out is your *expectations*. Your beliefs determine your expectations, your expectations determine your attitude, your attitude determines your actions, and your actions determine your results.

It starts with your values. Who are you really inside? What do you believe and care about? That determines your beliefs and your actions.

Act As If

Psychology has concluded that you can change your beliefs by practicing new thoughts and actions. It's called the *act as if principle*. You say, "I want to have purely positive beliefs. I want to have a belief that I am destined to be a great success in life. If that were true, how would I behave?"

The *Act As If Principle*: If 'x' were true, how would I behave?

Act as if you were already the person that you desire to be. These actions will create the feelings. The feelings will create the actions, which in turn will create the results.

You get rid of a self-limiting belief by replacing it with a positive, life-enhancing belief. You may say, "I don't believe in myself," or "I don't have enough confidence," or "I'm not smart enough, or attractive enough." Those are negative beliefs.

The positive belief is "I have more brainpower than I could ever use in my lifetime. It's just a matter of getting it out. I have the same unlimited ability to succeed that anybody else has. I'm an attractive and popular person. That's the belief that I choose to have." Then act as if you already had that belief. It wears down the old belief, which is eventually sent down to the basement, put in a box, and packed away. The new belief comes to dominate your life.

Although human beings are much more complex than computers, some people claim, "I can teach you how to reprogram your beliefs in hours or minutes." It's a quick-fix approach to reprogramming beliefs.

If it takes you a lifetime to develop a self-limiting belief, it's very doubtful that you will switch it in that short a time.

Even if, say, you consider yourself to be a loser in a sport and you win first place, that's not going to automatically cause you to see yourself as a winner for the rest of your life. You're going to backslide because of the comfort zone. You'll slip back into the old way of thinking.

When you do have a success, replay it in your mind. Before every event of importance, every person creates a visual picture of how they're going to perform. Sometimes it's clear, sometimes it's fuzzy, but it's always a visual picture. The person you see is the person you'll be.

So you can take a previous experience of success: you won a prize, you got an award. You still beam about how successful it was. You can then picture a coming event while remembering that happy event. That connects these two events in your subconscious mind, so you feel happy and confident about the upcoming event.

Athletes and performers do this all the time. Before they go on stage, they create a visual picture of themselves performing at their best. We call this *conditioning*.

One form of conditioning is used by all the top athletes in the world. Sitting quietly in a chair or lying in bed, they visualize themselves performing their sport perfectly. Figure skaters will put on the music they're going to skate by, and they'll mentally skate through their entire routine. They do this over and over before they go to sleep and get up in the morning. When they go out, they skate beautifully. They never fail, because they have pictured perfect skating. There are many stories about people who have never performed a sport before but are taught to visualize how to perform it and do a great job.

Everybody agrees with the statement that you become what you eat. Similarly—and Earl Nightingale called this "the strangest secret"—*you become what you think about most of the time.* If you think about yourself in positive, uplifting terms, that becomes your reality.

You become what you think about most of the time.
—Earl Nightingale, Legendary speaker

Fear of Rejection

The flip side of positive expectations is fear of rejection. Salespeople are often prone to this problem. They believe if they call someone, they're going to be rejected; the client is going to say, "No, I'm not interested" and slam down the phone. These salespeople dwell on those memories. They mentally replay the picture of the last person who was rude to them when they called. As they approach the telephone, they think about that and imagine there will be another rude person on the other end. Over time they become more and more fearful of calling, until finally they can't call at all. Most people drop out of sales not because of lack of success, but because they cannot take rejection. Rejection comes because they expect to be rejected.

It's just like the story I told about the gentlemen selling cellular telephones in a mall. After he'd been rejected ten or twenty or fifty times, he expected the next person to reject him as well. When he changed his thinking—no, this next person is going to buy from me, because this is a good deal, and they need it, and it will really help them—it transformed his behavior. It wasn't the product, it wasn't the customer, it wasn't the market. It was he himself who had this doubt, which came from the earlier rejection.

The way to build positive beliefs is by doing it. If you want to climb a mountain, climb one. For the rest of your life, you can say, "I climbed that mountain. Yes, I climb high mountains." For the rest of your life, you believe with 100 percent confidence that you can do it.

That's the key. You act your way into believing. You do the things that you would do if you already had the positive belief, and then it becomes automatic.

Martin Seligman and others are building what they call the *positive psychology field*. Thirty-five years ago, they called this *cognitive psychology*. This is another way of saying that you become what you think about most of the time. There's only one thing in the world that you can control, and that's your thinking. If you think about what you want, if you think about yourself as the best person you can be, and if you think about success and achievement, you will behave and perform accordingly.

As Napoleon Hill, author of *Think and Grow Rich*, said, "Whatever the mind of man can conceive and believe, it can achieve." That quote has transformed the lives of millions. If I believe something strongly enough and back it up with hard work, it becomes my reality. It becomes the truth for me, and it replaces all negative beliefs from the past.

Whatever the mind can conceive and believe, it can achieve.
—Napoleon Hill, author of *Think and Grow Rich*

Fear of Public Speaking

Studies show that most people fear public speaking more than death itself. Suppose a person has been promoted and now needs to do more public speaking, but is petrified, believing he is a terrible speaker. If he is going to succeed, he needs to develop a new belief about himself as an effective public speaker. What should this person do?

To begin with, everybody already *is* an effective public speaker. When you sit down with your friends or have a family get-together, you speak fluently, confidently, and clearly. People respond to you in a positive way. They laugh, joke, and give you feedback.

So one approach is to speak to others as if you're speaking to a family member across the dinner table. Or imagine you've seen a good movie, and you've sat down with a friend. You say, "Have you seen this movie?"

"No."

"Let me tell you about this movie. It's really good. I saw it last night. It was phenomenal."

When you speak in front of other people, imagine you're sharing some thoughts and experiences with family members across the dinner table. Never speak on a subject that you don't believe in or care about, because how you come across emotionally is going to connect with your audience.

Then plan and prepare. There's always an opening, a middle, and a close. Have a good opening, develop your talk with three key points, and have a close. Wrap it up by saying, "The most important thing I learned from this experience was this, and if I have learned it, you can too. Good luck."

Elbert Hubbard was one of the greatest authors in American history. I have his twenty-two volume series, in which he gave detailed stories of great orators, singers, explorers, adventurers, musicians, writers, poets, novelists, and military leaders. He wrote so prolifically that he had to buy a printing press to print all of his books. Even today, they're considered heirlooms.

People came to him and asked, "Mr. Hubbard, I want to be a great writer like you. What's the key?"

He would say, "The only way to learn to write is to write and write and write."

Similarly, the only way to learn to speak in public is to speak. Some say it takes 300 free talks before you will be able to give your first paid talk. The celebrated inspirational speaker Zig Ziglar said

---

**The only way to learn to speak—is to speak and speak. Every
time you do, your fears diminish and your confidence grows.**

---

he gave 3,000 free talks—mostly sales training for people in his
company—before he was ever invited to speak for money.

The only way to learn to speak is to speak and speak. Every
time you do, your fears diminish and your confidence grows.
Soon you reach the point where you are very confident. People
applaud you. They look up to you, shake your hand afterwards,
and say what a great message that was. Consequently, your fears
disappear. You now believe that you are a qualified and confident
speaker; if you're given enough time to plan and prepare, you can
do a great job, and everybody will be happy.

One Big Negative Belief

Everyone has one big negative belief which holds them back more
than anything else. Everyone has one big negative emotion, belief,
or idea, which is based on a previous experience or something that
someone said. Usually it's unclear. This is why in psychotherapy it
can take between six months and six years, meeting with a patient
once a week for fifty minutes, to identify what's holding them back.
Sometimes it takes a long time for a person to reach the point of
clarity and courage where they can tell the therapist, "This is my
problem. This is what happened to me. This is how I reacted."

But each person can become their own psychologist. Ninety-
nine percent of people do not need professional help. They need
the ability to think through and say, "What is the one big negative
idea or experience that's affecting my beliefs?"

Sometimes you can talk it out with your spouse, a good friend, a coach, or a minister. But until you can identify that one negative belief or experience that's holding you back, you're locked in place. As soon as you recognize it, you are liberated. Suddenly you're free, and it's gone forever.

FOUR

From Goal Setting to Goal Getting

Why are goals essential to success?

Imagine that you start off in life, as young people do, with a lot of confusion and uncertainty. Who am I? What do I do? Where do I go? What do I really want to do with my life?

When they're young, most people have no idea. I equate it to setting off across a strange country with no destination in mind, no road map, and no road signs. How long would it take you to get anywhere?

That's what 80 percent of the population do: they drive around and end up back at home every night. Eventually they decide there's nothing they can do. They've developed one of the most terrible of all human maladies: *learned helplessness.*

Learned helplessness is a major reason people don't succeed. They have not succeeded in the past, so they assume that, as Shakespeare said, "The past is prologue." They believe that what has happened in the past is what's going to happen in the future, so they lose their enthusiasm for goals.

I'll often ask my audiences, "How many people here have goals?" Every hand goes up. I say, "That's pretty surprising, because according to the studies, only 3 percent of people have goals. Everybody here has their hand up. So what are your goals?" They'll reply, "I want to be happy," "I want to be rich," or "I want to travel."

Many people don't have goals; they have wishes. A wish is a goal with no energy behind it. It's like a bullet with no powder in the cartridge. People go through life shooting blanks, because there's no energy behind their wishes.

If you think you have goals, you don't feel the need to set any. Some people even say you don't need them: all you need to do is listen to your heart, follow your instincts, and do whatever you feel like doing, and everything will come to you. I disagree. These people either are failures themselves or have already achieved success by setting and working on their goals aggressively for twenty-five years.

I know both types of people. I know wealthy people who say, "You don't really need to have goals. All you need to do is have happy thoughts and sit at home, and money will come to your mailbox." But at the beginning of their careers, they worked like dogs on their goals. They struggled, strived, sweated, and finally broke through.

Goals give you a track to run on; they give you a sense of direction, of clarity. They enable you to concentrate your energies and accomplish more in a year or two than many people do in five

---

**Goals give you a track to run on;
they give you a sense of direction, of clarity.**

---

or ten years. If you write down your goals and make plans to carry them out, you'll be astonished at how much more you accomplish, and how fast.

Seven Steps for Goal Setting

There are seven key steps for goal setting.

1. DECIDE WHAT YOU WANT, BE SPECIFIC

Sit down with a piece of paper and decide what you want. Decide exactly what you want to have in life without limitations. Imagine that you can have whatever you write down. The only limit is what you write down, clearly, on paper.

That's number one: *be specific*. Your goal should be so clear and specific that a six-year-old child could understand it and tell you how close you are. This is why "I want to be happy," "I want to be rich," "I want to travel" fail the goal test. Nobody could figure out what those mean. Are you there? How far away are you?

2. WRITE DOWN YOUR GOAL

Write down your goal where you can review it every day. A goal that is not in writing is only a fantasy; it's a wish, it's an illusion. When you write down a goal, you trigger your visual learning modality, because you see the goal. You trigger your audial modality because you say it subvocally to yourself, and you trigger your kinesthetic ability, because you are using the movement of your physical body to write it.

A number of studies have examined why students who take notes during class are vastly more successful than students who take no notes. When you're writing things down, you're transferring the written goal to your subconscious mind. Your subconscious mind is going to work before you even get up. It works twenty-four hours a day to bring that goal into your life. Writing down goals is one of the most extraordinary things I ever learned in my life.

3. SET A DEADLINE

Set a deadline to accomplish your goal. Set a specific date, and tell your subconscious mind that you want to achieve the goal by this time. If it's a long-term goal, break it down. If it's a five-year goal, break it down into five one-year goals. From a one-year goal, break it down into three-month goals, and then one-month goals, and then one-week goals. Many people, especially in sales and marketing, will break it down into one-day goals. Sometimes they'll break it down into one-hour goals: if I want to achieve this goal (say financial independence five years from now), this is what I'm going to have to do every hour of every day. They're very clear, and they discipline themselves to do what lies clearly at hand.

I love that quote from Thomas Carlyle: "Our great job in life is not to see what lies dimly at a distance, but to do what lies clearly at hand." Successful people do what lies clearly at hand. They do the most important thing now, they get it done, and they get on with it. Unsuccessful people have excuses to procrastinate. They check their email, send a text, or talk to someone while having a cup of coffee. In the back of their minds they mean well; they have good intentions. What is the road to hell paved with? Good intentions.

As the economist Ludwig von Mises said, "Only action is action. Not talk, not wish, not hope, not intention. Only action is action."

"Only action is action. Not talk, not wish, not hope, not intention. Only action is action." —Ludwig Von Mises, Economist

---

4. MAKE A LIST

Step number four is to *make a list* of everything that you could possibly do to achieve the goal. Keep adding to the list until it is complete.

There's something about writing down every step that transforms your thinking. Let's say your goal is to double your income. "Holy smokes—I'm going to double my income in twelve months?" It's enormous, but then you ask, "What would I need to do to double my income?" You begin to write things down: "I need to upgrade my skills in this area, or I need to read this book, or go to this course. These are the things I'd have to do every day if I wanted to upgrade my knowledge and skills and achieve my goal." Just keep writing them down. You'll be astonished.

5. ORGANIZE A PLAN

Step number five is, *you take your list and you organize the list into a plan.* You organize your list into a plan by creating a checklist. Checklists are one of the great miracles of modern success. People who use them accomplish five or ten times as much as people who don't.

This is a list of every single step in order. What is step number one to achieve my goal? What is step number two; what is step number three?

I was giving a seminar in Sydney, Australia, and a young entrepreneur, who was about twenty-six years old, came up to me and said, "I don't know how to achieve my goal."

"What is your goal?"

"I want to sell my business. I started this business when I was nineteen. I've been working at it now for seven years. It's successful, it makes good money, but I've always wanted to travel and see the world. I'm twenty-six, and I don't want to work for the rest of my life. I'm still single. I want to sell my business and travel."

"What have you done?"

"I talk to people, I ask people; I just don't know."

"Why don't you go to the bookstore and get a book on how to sell your business? Many entrepreneurs have written about that."

"Are there books on this subject?"

"Absolutely. Tens of thousands of businesses are sold every year by successful entrepreneurs to others who want to pick up and carry on."

At the lunch break, the young man went across the street to a bookstore and bought two books on how to sell your business.

He said, "I've never seen this stuff: how you put together financial statements, how you advertise, how you position, how you find interest groups and different industries."

Two months later, he wrote me a letter saying, "I sold my business. I got a great price. I have all the money I need. My ticket is paid for. I'm leaving for Europe. I'm going to see the world. It was amazing."

If you want to sell your business, the first thing to do is get a book on how to sell a business. If you want to double your sales, get a book on how to increase your sales. If you want to manage your time better, get a book on that subject.

6. TAKE THE FIRST STEP

Step number six is *take the first step*. It's like pushing off when you're skiing. Suddenly you're in motion, you're moving forward, you're gaining speed and going faster. Momentum kicks in, and you get a feeling of progress. You become exhilarated.

All success comes from taking the first step. As Confucius said, "A journey of a thousand leagues begins with a single step."

Yet taking the first step is the hardest thing of all.

Sometimes I ask my audiences, "How many people have books at home that they've bought and intend to read someday?" Everybody. "Here's what you do," I say. "Go back, pick up the book, and read the first chapter. If that doesn't get you going into the book, it's fine; you've given it your best shot."

Ninety percent of business books are not read beyond the first chapter. Why is that? Because after reading the first chapter, people decide that this is not that helpful, it's not that good, it's not that well-written. Read the first chapter. It transforms your life to take the first step. All success comes from taking the first step.

7. ACT TOWARD YOUR GOAL

Step number seven in goal setting is, *do something every day on your major goal*. Do something every day, whether it's small or large, to move toward your goal. Read something, learn something, do something, but every day keep the plate spinning, keep the momentum going, keep moving.

The momentum principle of success also says that if you stop moving towards your goal, it's hard to start moving again. But if you keep moving towards your goal, it's much easier to keep moving. It's one of the greatest of all principles of success: continuous motion.

The 7 Key Steps for Goal Setting

1. Decide what you want; *be specific.*
2. Write down your goal where you can review it every day.
3. Set a deadline to accomplish your goal.
4. Make a list of everything you could do to achieve the goal.
5. Take the list and organize it into a plan.
6. Take the first step.
7. Do something every day to move toward your goal.

An Exercise for Goal Setting

Take a clean sheet of paper and write down ten goals that you would like to accomplish in the next twelve months. Twelve-month goals are more powerful than two-, or five-, or ten-year goals. You can write on another sheet of paper that you want to make a million dollars in ten years; that's fine. But keep the focus on twelve months, which you can focus on.

Your subconscious mind is like a child: it's simple, it's innocent, and it can only accept commands that are very simple.

Write down ten goals using the three P's: *personal, positive,* and in the *present* tense. The first P is *personal,* so you always begin a goal with the word *I. I earn, I achieve, I sell, I drive, I live in.* Whatever the goal is, it's *I* plus an action verb. That's what activates your subconscious mind and starts it to work like an engine.

Step number two is make it *positive.* Never say *I stop smoking, I quit smoking, I stop doing this,* or *I lose this number of pounds.* Always say *I weigh this number of pounds* and so on.

Step number three is state your goal in the *present tense*, because your subconscious mind cannot process a command unless it's in the present tense. So you say *I earn this amount of money* and then write *by this date. I earn this amount of money by December 31. I weigh this number of pounds by this date, at the end of a particular month.* Your subconscious mind loves time pressure. It goes to work twenty-four hours a day to move you toward the goal and attract it to you.

I've taught this to more than a million people in seventy-five countries. They come back to me years later and say, "You changed my life. You made me rich. I was struggling, I was going nowhere, I was in debt, I was broke, I lost my job, and then you changed my life, you made me rich."

"What did this?" I ask.

"It was the goals." It was always that exercise.

I gave this exercise to a very wealthy man recently. After I left, he wrote down ten goals. He later said, "The goals started to materialize almost as I was writing. The phone rang, people came in. It was miraculous." He could not believe how fast the goals were achieved. They were one-year goals, but they started to be reached almost immediately.

Sometimes people say, "What if it doesn't work?"

No, that's the wrong question. The right question is, what if it *does* work? It just cost you a piece of paper, a pen, and five minutes of your time. Is that so much?

Another exercise: Imagine that you have a magic wand that will enable you to achieve any one goal on your list within twenty-four hours. What one goal, if you achieved it, would have the greatest positive impact? What one goal would change your life more than anything else?

A person wants to have a big house, but what would enable them to have a big house? A certain level of income. You say, "I earn this amount of money so that I can have this house."

Start off with the one goal that would have the biggest positive impact on all your other goals. Put a circle around that, then take a clean sheet of paper and write it down. Positive, present tense, personal: *I achieve this goal by this date.* Then make a list of everything you can do to achieve that one goal.

Then organize this list by sequence. What do you do first? What do you second? Then take action on your list; do something every day.

If I could only give people one piece of advice, it would be to write down your goals in this way.

As I've said, accepting personal responsibility is the starting point of becoming an adult. Until you accept responsibility, you're still a child; you're still blaming all your problems on someone else. When you cross the line and accept responsibility, you become an adult for the first time.

Responsibility for what? Responsibility for your goals.

When you cross the line and accept responsibility for your goals, you become an adult for the first time.

Reinvention

Let's say you are somebody who has achieved something significant at a young age, but you lose your motivation later on. Many actors who gain great fame in their teens are broke and addicted to drugs by the time they're forty. Many athletes who have retired are broke or have committed suicide by the age of fifty.

I've written a book called *Reinvention*. It talks about what you do when your life changes, when there's turmoil, when your career ends, or your industry ends. How do you reinvent yourself?

You go back to writing down your goals. What would I do if my life were perfect? What would I do differently from today? Where do I want to be in five or ten years?

Ninety-five percent of actors and actresses are unemployed at any given time. To get a job is a tremendous break. You must know the right people, you must be in the right time at the right place, you must take hundreds of bit parts and be discovered to get a slightly bigger part. You must play that part so well that you're given a supporting role. Even so, it's possible that you won't work for another five years.

Many actors haven't had a job for five years, but their expenses continue. James Caan got an Academy Award for *The Godfather.* He became very selective and turned down some of the best roles in Hollywood. He was the first choice for *Tootsie,* which went on to win two Academy Awards. He turned down a couple of these roles, and he ended up living in a one-bedroom apartment with two dogs in Hollywood, because he had run out of money. If you don't have any money, they don't invite you to parties. If you're not in roles, they don't invite you. You can't take any trips, and you just keep going out day after day, week after week, auditioning for a part, any part, because it's the only way you have to make money.

In show business, people's careers sometimes fade when they irritate somebody who puts a black mark on them, and nobody else will hire them. The only skill that got you out of the ditch is your ability to act, and there's no work. Of course in the entertainment industry, you're surrounded with drugs. You can get drugs as easily as chewing gum. Then people learn that this guy's on drugs: they don't touch him with a ten-foot pole. If you're going to invest millions of dollars in a movie, you can't risk having one of the actors not show up. So their career just goes into the ditch.

Most actors and actresses are fighting with self-esteem issues. They're trying to compensate for what happened to them as children by earning the adulation of strangers. These people will crawl over broken glass to please their audiences, but then they become arrogant, condescending, and ridiculous.

In sports, even if people are successful, their bodies only last for a certain period of time. They've never developed any other skills, so there's nothing they can do. Some athletes do plan for their later lives: they put money aside and invest carefully. They've already begun making their transition plans. When their career comes to an end, they're ready. They've got new opportunities; they have job offers.

With entrepreneurs, on the other hand, you rarely hear of drug addiction, alcoholism, or declining into apathy. Why? Because they're so busy all the time. They're active; they have goals. They're taking steps forward, they're accomplishing things, they're changing from product to product and company to company.

I'm sure that there are lots of drugs in the high-tech world, but you don't hear about people who make a lot of money there falling apart and become hopeless drug addicts. They're doing new things. They've got this mindset: *I succeeded, and I succeeded based on my own hard efforts. I succeeded in competition with thousands of other people, and I want to compete.* They're surrounded by people who are positive, upbeat and motivated, who have goals and energy.

You seldom see an entrepreneur who becomes successful and then falls apart. I've met entrepreneurs who are billionaires and multi-billionaires. All they think about is the next business, the next opportunity, the next product, the next service. They don't fall apart and drink.

The thing that keeps you going is having something to look forward to. This is the most important thing in life. Without it, people lose hope. And hope is the great motivator of the human being—hope for a better future through your own efforts.

One way to turn up the volume on your self-esteem is simply to repeat "I like myself" enthusiastically and with conviction. When you get up in the morning, say, "I like myself, and I love my work. I like myself; I love my work." You can't say this for more than a few seconds without starting to smile and having blood pour into your brain, releasing endorphins. Positive self-talk, or affirmations, is extraordinarily powerful.

The average person speaks to themselves in an inner dialogue of about 1,500 words a minute. It flows like a fast moving river. If you are not careful, that inner dialogue will be negative. You'll talk about things you're mad at or worried about, people that you're irritated with, and so on.

The default setting on every human brain is to think about their worries and pains. You have to click the default setting off by talking to yourself about who you want to be and what you want to accomplish. Step into the dialogue, deliberately stop it, and speak positively to yourself.

**Hope is the great motivator of the human being—
hope for a better future through your own efforts.**

Seven Steps to Success

Here is a seven-step process for increasing your income ten times in ten years. In fact, people all over the world who learned that process have told me that it didn't take ten years; it took five or six. Ten was far too conservative.

The formula is very simple.

1. Get up every morning an hour early and read to upgrade your skills. Wealthy people read an hour or two every day. Poor people don't read at all, except maybe newspapers.

2. Write down your goals every single day in a spiral notebook. Every day, without looking at the previous page, rewrite your major goals to reprogram them into your mind.

3. Plan every day in advance. You'll increase your productivity 25 percent by simply making a list of everything you need to do before you start.

4. Focus and concentrate on your most important task. You'll increase your productivity by 50–100 percent by starting and completing your most important task first thing every day. It's one of the greatest success principles in history.

5. After every single event of importance, do an after-action report: *What did I do right? What would I do differently?* If you do that and capture your experience on paper, you'll increase your learning speed by about five or ten times. When you write down your answers, you program them into your subconscious mind, and they become part of your permanent operating system.

6. Listen to audio programs all the time you can. You can now have hundreds of hours of the best audio learning in the world. Instead of listening to music, turn driving time into learning

time. Turn your car into a university on wheels. Never stop taking in new information.

7. Treat everyone you meet as though they're the most important person in the world. Treat them with grace, respect, pleasantness, cordiality, geniality, and courtesy. Be nice to people. The most successful people in the world are described by others as nice people. Just do that, and every door of opportunity will open up to you.

Get Going and Keep Going

Orison Swett Marden, a businessman in the 1890s, decided to write a book on success because so many people were succeeding; America was booming.

Marden had lost his business and his money, and he was living in a room over a stable. When he finished his book, he was so happy that he went down the street to treat himself to a beer and a steak dinner. While he was eating, he heard shouting in the street and a fire alarm. The stable burned to the ground, and his entire manuscript was gone. He was completely destitute. He moved to another city, got another job, and rewrote the book from memory.

This was in the early 1890s. By the time he had finished rewriting his book, the country had gone into a depression. Nobody was interested in it now.

Marden was at a meeting where someone said, "Somebody should write about these success principles so we can get this country going again."

"I've written a book like that," said Marden, "but I haven't been able to find a publisher."

The other man said, "I've got a couple of publisher friends. Let's take a look at the manuscript."

The publisher said, "This is great stuff." Published under the title *Pushing to the Front*, it became the best-selling book in America. Eight hundred pages long, it is one of the greatest success books ever written. Some have said it was the book that single-handedly brought America into the twentieth century.

In the 1890s, Marden founded *Success* magazine, and he wrote a series of other books on success. If you can find them today, they're mind-blowing. They're some of the best books on personal and business success ever written.

Marden's advice was simple: "get going and keep going"—*get-to-itiveness* and *stick-to-itiveness.*

Review of The 7 Steps to Success

1. Get up an hour early every day and read to upgrade your skills.
2. Write down your goals every single day in a spiral notebook.
3. Plan every day in advance.
4. Focus and concentrate on your most important task.
5. After every single event of importance, ask *What did I do right? What would I do differently?*
6. Listen to audio programs all the time you can.
7. Treat everyone you meet as though they are the most important person in the world.

FIVE

Right Action and Flexibility

Taking action towards your goals is the single most important quality of all. The world is full of talented people with fantasies and dreams, but they don't act. They always have an excuse not to do it yet.

When you take action, three things happen:

1. You get immediate feedback from your actions, which enable you to change course and direction.
2. You get ideas for more actions to move ahead faster.
3. Your self-confidence and self-esteem go up.

You get all three of those benefits from taking action, and you get nothing from sitting there on the couch.

Once you have decided to achieve a goal, the first action will appear almost like a light on the floor in a nightclub. You can always see the first step. It will always be clear. If you take it, the second step will appear, and if you take that, the third step will appear.

Here's an interesting discovery: nothing works, at least not for the first time. When you take action toward a goal, be assured that it's not going to work at first. Peter Drucker says that you need at least four iterations in your direction toward a new goal before you hit the right one, but that was, I think, in the old days. According to a study in *Harvard Business Review*, one company tried fifteen different business models before they found the one that worked. Another business made thirty-four changes in their business model before it hit. One very successful business did ninety-nine different iterations in their startup.

The only thing that matters is, does it work; is it getting you the results that you expected? People can fall in love with a course of action even before it's worked. Peter Drucker said, "If the American public knew how many mistakes were made in the management suite because of managerial ego, there would be riots in the streets."

The critical thing is to act and then get feedback. Get an idea, act, fail fast, learn quickly, try again. Repeat: get an idea, try it out, get feedback, make a mistake, learn, and try it again. It's an endless cycle. Jim Collins, author of *Good to Great*, calls it "the doom loop." Keep making mistakes and learning lessons, and finally the process starts to move faster and faster. Every successful person has made an enormous number of mistakes. You start off with a direction, take your first step, move toward the goal, and get feedback. You then use that feedback to change your course of action.

Try, learn, change. Try, learn, change. Ego, learned helplessness, and the comfort zone are all fighting against us, so we often try something and give up if it doesn't work: "It must have been the wrong idea." No, try it again. Keep adjusting. This is why flexibility is so important. As Charles Darwin observed, "Survival

---

"Get an idea, act, fail fast, learn quickly, try again." —Brian Tracy

---

goes not necessarily to the strongest or most intelligent of the species, but to the one most adaptable to change."

Back in the nineties, a major institute in New York did a study to discover the most important quality for success in the twenty-first century. The researchers looked at many qualities—vision, courage, ambition, persistence, innovation—but they found the number one quality was flexibility in the face of changing circumstances.

How do you know you need to be flexible, you need to adapt and change your course of action? The answer is, it's not working. You're not getting the results that you expected. Back to the drawing board.

Lessons from the Bamboo Tree

The website Presentation Zen lists seven lessons from the bamboo tree in the Japanese forest and what it can teach us about being flexible in today's modern world.

The first is, *a bamboo tree bends, but it doesn't break.* It's flexible, yet it's firmly rooted.

Harvard did a study among several hundred CEOs, asking them about their biggest failures and how they coped with failure. They got blank looks from most of them, who said, "We've never failed in this company."

"Yes, but you launched this product or this service, and it didn't work."

"No, those weren't failures," they said. "Those were just learning experiences. We never fail. We just learn things."

Some of those experiences were expensive and painful, but leaders always look at a situation that way.

To go back to the bamboo tree, the roots are the unshakable belief that you are going to be successful sooner or later, and that this is just a short-term setback. Whatever's happening to you, if it's not working out, that's fine. Take a deep breath, step back, and do something else.

Nevertheless, there is a big difference between flexibility and compromising on core principles. The studies show that leaders are very clear about their values, and they never compromise them. I've written twenty books on management, and I've read thousands more, and it always comes down to the same thing: integrity. Integrity means remaining consistent with your values.

Entrepreneur Guy Kawasaki says that the first thing to do when you start a business is sit down with the key people and ask, "What do we believe in? What are our fundamental values? What are the unshakable principles that we're going to work by?"

Usually the principles are very simple, and there are not more than three to five. They're things like absolute integrity, internally and externally; high-quality products; a commitment to customer service; a commitment to developing people; or having good results with people. You organize them in sequence: the most important principle always comes first and governs the next ones. Similarly, the second principle dominates the lower principles. In one great company I worked with, profitability was number five.

Your preeminent value takes precedence over all the others. Say your desire for success, to earn a lot of money, is very high, but your fear of failure and making a mistake is slightly higher. The more intense emotion will dominate the less intense emotion. So pick, and organize, your values.

Imagine you meet two men at a party, each of whom has the same values. The first man's values are, in order, family, health, and success. The second man has the same three values, but in this order: success, family, and health.

Would there be a difference between these two men? There would be an enormous difference. Someone who puts family ahead of success or anything else is going to be a very different person from a person who puts success ahead of everything else.

I remember a friend I used to have. He was married, with children—a nice guy, very successful, very smart. We were at his home. There were about six or eight of us there, couples, and we were talking about business. He said, "I know one thing for sure. My financial success takes precedence over my family or anything else." I looked at his wife. She had a flat, cold, shocked look on her face.

Before it was over, she had died of cancer, primarily caused by stress, the son was an alcoholic, the daughter had gotten pregnant and moved away, and the man ended up broke with a second wife. He moved to a small town in Arizona, where he lives to this day. Brilliant, bright, smart, but every single time push came to shove, the money came first, not the friendship, not the reputation, not anything else.

So it's really important to think about what your values are; they are your roots. There are many values that you can have, but the two most important ones are to accept responsibility and always tell the truth. If you have those two, all the other values will fall into place naturally.

It's really important to think about what your values are; they are your roots.

What Looks Weak Is Strong

The second principle of the bamboo tree is that *what looks weak is strong*. Bamboo doesn't look impressive, but it endures cold winters and extremely hot summers, and it will be the only tree left standing after a typhoon. How can you relate that idea to an individual being flexible in life?

Jim Collins' book *Good to Great* looked at companies that had been merely average for a long time and then became great companies, world leaders. He found that for each one of them, the turning point on the road to greatness was appointing what he called a "Level 5 leader." A Level 5 leader was not someone in the newspapers, in the press, or on the talk shows. This person was usually very calm and easygoing, loved the business, had a tremendous commitment to its success, and had very high moral values as well. These spread out through the entire company— quality people, relationships, customers, products, and services, and an absolute determination and commitment to excellence.

This outlook transformed these companies. Some of them became the greatest companies of the world. In addition, they were the most flexible in every economic situation. They always had cash reserves. They always were willing to change their strategy. They always were willing to pull back if the economy shrank. So they keep going strong—big, highly respected, and profitable, year after year.

Be Always Ready

The third quality of the bamboo tree is, *it's always ready*. Bamboo needs little processing or finishing. In this case, it means to be continually learning. You should be current with everything that's going on in your field.

Charlie Munger, who is Warren Buffett's right-hand man and a multi-billionaire as a result, has said, "If you're not continually learning and growing in the world of today, you're not going to have a chance in the future."

Warren Buffett and Carlos Slim are two of the richest men in the world. They spend 80 percent of their time reading. They people read and read and learn and learn. They fill their minds with new information and ideas on the areas that are important to their businesses. As a result, they make brilliant decisions. They buy into industries that nobody was looking at. It's always a front-page story: "Buffett buys this or that company." It turned out that this company had hidden assets and a tremendous potential to be made far more profitable. Nobody else had seen it, but Buffett got those insights from reading, study, and talking to people.

I have one seminar called the Two Day MBA, which is a crash course in practical business management. I have another seminar called Business Model Reinvention. It's also a two-day crash course. It covers twelve parts of a business model and gives a profit model for any business. It shows you that if your profits are down for any reason, it means that one of these elements in the system is broken or obsolete. Whatever you were doing before to generate profits is not working.

I give people these ideas, and 80 percent of them go back and transform their businesses. Who is at these seminars? The best businesspeople in every community—the top managers, the top entrepreneurs, the most successful people, whose time is really valuable. They're there, they're in front, and they're taking notes, because they recognize that if they don't keep upgrading their skills, they're going to fall behind.

Spring Back

The fourth quality of the bamboo tree is, *unleash your power to spring back*. One of the most important qualities for success is resilience: the ability to bounce back.

You are only as free as your well-developed options. If you have only one choice, if there's only one job you can do, you're trapped. If something changes and you lose a job or your skill becomes obsolete, you may go home and not work for two or three years.

The only way to develop more options is by keeping and developing new skills. That will give you flexibility, options, and the power to spring back.

Another thing that's really important is sleep. Adequate sleep is essential for proper brain functioning. You recharge your cell phone when the battery's in the red. You need to recharge your mental battery as well. If you're reading this book, chances are that you're a knowledge worker. You don't work with your body, making and moving things; you work with your brain. The most important thing you can do is to keep your brain fully charged.

A recent study found that non-millionaires sleep six or seven hours a night. The richest people get 8.46 hours, and they get up before 6:00 a.m. That means they've got to go to bed by nine.

When you do this, you have much more resilience. No matter what happens, you're calm and relaxed. You're not tired, irritable, or frustrated, or thinking about going back to bed. I sometimes ask my audiences, "How many people here who, when you got

---

You're only as free as your well-developed options.

---

up in the morning, immediately thought about when you could go back to bed tonight?" Fifty percent of the audience raise their hands. I say, "That means that you're not getting enough sleep." They're running with a sleep deficit.

I advise my clients, "Go to bed at 9:00, turn everything off, and get eight, nine, even ten hours of sleep." They come back transformed. They've got more energy. They've lost weight. Because if you're not getting enough sleep, you eat too much to compensate. You drink too much coffee, you take too many soft drinks, and at night you drink a whole bottle of wine. You're doing anything possible to get yourself pumped, because you're tired all the time.

As soon as my clients start getting eight and a half or nine hours of sleep at night, they become more effective and earn more money. Sometimes they triple their income in the first ninety days. They're healthier, more personable with their families, more influential and persuasive with others. Their senses of humor are better and they make better business decisions.

To unleash your power to spring back, get lots of rest. If you do, you can endure almost anything. If you're tired and irritable, you're going to overreact, say things you'll regret, and make decisions that will be very expensive to correct in the future.

Sometimes the best use of your time is not to get caught up or get more things done. It's to come home early, go to bed, and sleep the whole night. You'll do better work and make fewer mistakes. In two or three hours, you can do what may take you eight hours if you're tired and dragging, and it will be much better work. It's a great payoff. You don't lose. You actually gain time and productivity by being well rested.

Sitting Alone

The fifth principle is to *find wisdom in emptiness.* The hollow insides of bamboo reminds us that we are often too full of ideas and conclusions to embrace new knowledge.

Your intuition has a great capacity for guiding you unerringly to do and say the right thing. Emerson called this "the still, small voice within." But in order to tap into your intuition, you have to create zones of silence. Mindfulness is a big subject now. People are taking five-day retreats and paying thousands of dollars to learn how to be mindful. But all you really have to do is sit in the silence.

A person begins to become great when they begin to listen to their inner voice. The way to do this is to put aside everything—no cigarettes, magazines, or music—and sit quietly by yourself for at least thirty to sixty minutes.

It's like a bucket of muddy water: your brain takes about twenty-four to twenty-six minutes to clear. In this time, you'll have an irresistible impulse to get up and do something. Just stay there, and you'll suddenly become calm and clear, and your mind will start to become almost enlightened. Then the answer to the biggest problem that you're facing will coast into your mind. The message will be clear, like a great billboard. But this only works if you practice solitude on a regular basis.

The French philosopher Blaise Pascal said, "All of humanity's problems stem from man's inability to sit quietly in a room alone." Instead, people go out and start wars and revolutions.

> "All of humanity's problems stem from man's inability to sit quietly in a room alone." —Blaise Pascal, philosopher

People who sit quietly and let their minds clear are much calmer and more creative. They make better decisions, they're much more personable, they have much lower flash points, and they don't get angry very much. They smile a lot and remain calm.

One of the most important things you can do for success is to do nothing for thirty to sixty minutes each day. This has particular value today, when silence has become increasingly rare. Everywhere you go are TVs and other forms of noise pollution. Unless we are out in nature or intentionally silence ourselves, we can hardly hear our inner voice.

Continuous Growth

The sixth principle of the bamboo tree is to *commit to continuous growth*. Bamboo trees are among the fastest-growing plants in the world, but when farmers plant the bamboo trees, they put in the seeds and water, and nothing happens. They do this month after month. A year goes by, and nothing happens. They keep doing this for five years, and still nothing happens. In that time, the bamboo tree has been developing a very deep root system. And then the tree grows 100 feet and becomes one of the strongest plants in the world, but it can hold that 100 feet of weight only thanks to its deep root system.

It's the same thing when you are learning, growing, and developing new knowledge and skills. Remember: one idea can change your life. But you never know what the idea is, so you must be continually taking in lots of new ideas so that the right one will come to you at the right time.

I'll give you an example. I was listening to an interview with a successful entrepreneur, who was asked, "What's the key to being successful in business?"

"Ninety percent of business success," he replied, "is determined by the quality of the product in the first place."

I almost drove off the road when I heard that. I've seen this principle repeated a thousand times, but the way it was phrased—90 percent of business success is determined by the quality of the product in the first place—struck me.

I developed an entire two-day seminar around this concept: How do you develop and sell a truly excellent product? How do you know that it is excellent? Where do you get the necessary people, skills, techniques, and customer service?

Every successful company triggers the same reaction from the customer: "This is a great product. Those are great people. This is a great place." I ask business owners, "What percentage of your customers, after using your product or service, turn to you and say, 'This is a great product'? That percentage is the single factor that determines your future in business. The percentage of people who say, 'This is a great product' determines your entire future."

This all may seem obvious, but is it true for you as a person? Your success, income, promotion, and lifestyle will be determined by the quality of your work. Your job is to get into the top 10 percent in your field. It's not like the Olympics, where the goal is to be number one. You just have to be in the top 10 percent, because that top 10 percent, among both companies and individuals, earn 90 percent of the income that's distributed in any society.

Your goal should be to get into the top 10% in your field.

What does it take to get into the top 10 percent? The decision to get there. Nobody can stop you from being in the top 10 percent, from being recognized as a high-quality producer of your product or service.

Is it easy to get there? No. How long does it take? According to Malcolm Gladwell in *Outliers*, citing work on elite performance, it takes five to seven years. According to Jim Collins' *Good to Great*, the Level 5 leader, the strong, calm, effective leader, took over five to seven years to take the company from being merely good to being a world leader.

Set that as your goal: "I want people to say that he's one of the best in the business." The top doctors who are recognized as such earn $80,000 or $100,000 a day, while the average doctors out in the suburbs are getting $150 a visit. They all went to the same medical schools, but the doctors—especially the surgeons—who dedicated themselves to excelling at their craft pulled ahead. They got further and further ahead of the average. Their income didn't go up by 10 percent or 20 percent. It went up by ten or twenty *times*. It all comes from continual personal development, getting a little bit better every day.

Usefulness through Simplicity

The seventh principle: *express usefulness through simplicity*. The bamboo tree expresses its usefulness in its simplicity.

Success doesn't require enormous complexity. There's been a lot of work done on reengineering: how do you reengineer a business, or, for that matter, a personal life? The answer is to stop doing things. The companies that were most successful in the last recession were the ones that *stopped* doing the most things. Not the ones that started the greatest number of new things—the ones that stopped doing things that weren't working that well.

Ask, "Is there anything that I'm doing today that I wouldn't get into again? It may have seemed like a good idea at the time, but knowing what I now know, I wouldn't get into it again."

If you find that you would not get into this enterprise knowing what you know now, get out fast. Don't delay; don't procrastinate. If you have a person on staff that you would not hire again, let them go today. If you have a product that you would not bring to the market today, discontinue it. Cut it off.

Often the senior executive who got the company into trouble is not capable of getting it out, because there's too much ego involvement in previous products and decisions. As a result, the board of directors brings in a turnaround artist. The turnaround artist has no emotional involvement. Usually, they're brought in for one year, maybe less, and they come in with a chainsaw.

Review of 7 Lessons of The Bamboo Tree

1. A bamboo tree bends, but it doesn't break.
2. What looks weak is strong.
3. It's always ready.
4. Unleash your power to spring back.
5. Find wisdom in emptiness.
6. Commit to continuous growth.
7. Express usefulness through simplicity.

In fact, one of the most famous turnaround artists was called "Chainsaw Dunlap." He could take a Fortune 500 company that was losing money and turn it around within twelve months. They'd give him a big, fat bonus, and he'd walk off. There would be bodies everywhere. They'd bring in a new president, and the company would restructure and become successful and profitable.

Be your own turnaround artist. The key to success is to *stop* doing things.

Be your own turnaround artist.
The key to success is to *stop* doing things.

Reengineering

This brings us to reengineering, which is based on reducing the number of steps in any given process. Andrew Grove wrote about this in *High Output Management* many years ago. His advice: make a careful list of all the steps in any process, then eliminate 30 percent of them. Sit down with the people involved and ask, "How can we eliminate these steps?" There are a number of approaches:

1. Eliminate the step completely. Many steps have gotten in because of an emergency or a mistake.
2. Consolidate two steps or three steps together.
3. Discontinue that process or part of that process.
4. Outsource the process to another company, which can do it better than you can.

The first time, you shrink the number of steps by 30 percent. Then you go back and do it again.

When Steve Jobs came back to Apple in 1997, he found that the company was ninety days from insolvency. They had thousands of people selling 104 products all over the world. He said, "We've got to stop the bleeding." He had every top executive come in and recommend ten products that they would continue with. All the others would be dropped.

People shouted and screamed, but each manager came in with their lists, and they consolidated them until they had a consensus of ten products that they would keep.

"Now," said Jobs, "in the next few days I want you to go home, have discussions, and eliminate six more."

Of course the executives were shocked, but Jobs said, "It's either this or closing the company. Please understand your jobs are at stake here, as well as the jobs of thousands of other people."

The managers sulked and blustered, and some resigned, but in the end, they cut 100 products out of 104. The whole company turned around. Within a few years, Apple became the most valuable company in the world by discontinuing products with low growth, low income, or low profit.

So when you get overwhelmed in your life, sit down and say, "What do I need to stop doing?" Then stop. Cut it off now.

Salespeople can even do this with clients that provide them with little in sales or profits. They can cut them, keeping the most profitable 20 percent.

Errant Assumptions

Peter Drucker once said that errant assumptions lie at the root of all failures. We're assuming something that's not true; we're assuming that there's a market that either does not exist, is not big enough, or is not profitable enough. We're assuming that a person will become a good producer, although people never change.

The starting point is to question your assumptions and ask: what if I was wrong? What if my assumptions in this area, about the product, the service, the people, the market, the customers, were completely wrong? What would I do then?

I teach some basic questions in my business courses:

1. What am I trying to do? Be clear. The answer is, you're trying to get business results—meaning that you're going to earn an excess of profits over all the costs involved.

2. How am I trying to do it? Always ask this question when you're experiencing frustration, resistance, low performance, struggle, stress, anger, or dissatisfaction with your work. Stop the clock and ask, "What am I trying to do, and how am I trying to do it?" When people do that, they realize that they've tried to do something in the same way for five years, and it still hasn't worked.

3. Is there a better way? Could there be a better way than the one we're using today? (There always is.) Knowing what we now know, would we start to do it this way again? What would we do differently? That keeps your mind open.

These questions are like slapping people in the face. What are we trying to do? How are we trying to do it? Is it working? If not, why not? What are our assumptions? What would we do if our assumptions were wrong? What if we had no limitations? What if we had an unlimited budget and we could do anything we wanted? What would we do differently if they were to come in and shoot us in the head if we hadn't accomplished the goal in six months? What changes would we make immediately? Put the pressure on, and people come up with incredible ideas.

SIX

The Importance of Daily Self-Talk

I've already mentioned the power of suggestion in determining everything that happens to you. You're greatly influenced by both external influences and internal influences. You can only respond and react to external influences, but you need to take complete control of your internal influences, because they're far greater.

One thing that revolutionized my life was this very simple principle: with affirmations and positive self-talk, your future and your potential are unlimited, because 95 percent of your emotions are determined by how you talk to yourself on an ongoing basis. You become what you think about most of the time. You also become what you say to yourself most of the time.

What words do you say to yourself? Remember that the default setting in the human brain is to talk to yourself in a negative way, to see the worst. You think about your worries, your pains, and your grievances, because these are the thorns in your side.

Seldom do we deliberately choose to think about the things that we like and that make us happy. As you talk to yourself in a

---

Remember that the default setting in the human brain is to talk to yourself in a negative way. Take control of your inner dialogue and choose to think in a positive way.

---

positive way, as you take control of this inner dialogue that's continuously going night and day (even while you're asleep), you take control of your emotions. As you do, you take control of your attitude. You also begin to change your beliefs and your expectations.

The greatest single obstacle to success is the fear of failure, the fear of loss. What if I lose my job? What if I lose my money? What if I lose my time? What if I lose the love of someone else?

This is always manifested in the feeling *I can't. I can't change, I can't do this, I can't improve things.* It's learned helplessness.

What is the antidote to this fear of failure? The answer is, *I can do it.* Instead of saying, *I can't* and becoming angry, you say, *I can, I can do it, I can do anything I put my mind to.*

Fortunately, you can go back and reprogram an upbringing of negativity by repeating these words over and over again: *I like myself. I like myself. I like myself.* This drives the idea deeper into your subconscious mind, like pilings used to build a bridge, and eventually cancels out any negative programming.

When parents are raising children, they keep saying, *stop, get away from that, don't do that, don't touch that.* This is in order to protect the child, but the child, who is driven by its natural instincts to explore its environment, only hears, *I'm too small, I'm incompetent, I'm incapable, I can't.* At a very early age children stop exploring and trying new things because they know that their parents are going to get mad at them.

Shampoo in the Jacuzzi

The child's greatest fear is the fear of loss of a parent's love. That's why the greatest gift of a parent is unconditional love—when they make it clear that they love their children and back them 100 percent, no matter what they do or say.

Once I got an emergency call from my country club. My son David and his friend, who were about ten or eleven years old, had gone over there and were playing around. They got some shampoo from the locker room and put it in the Jacuzzi outside.

The Jacuzzi frothed up, and people came running. The management came out and called the police. Then they called us. We drove over there. There were two police cruisers. You'd think there'd been a massive robbery, but it was just this Jacuzzi foaming up.

My son and his friend were petrified. I asked the police, "What's happening?"

"Kids are just kids; they got a big scare. The country club's making too much of this, but we have to stand by like there's a serious crime in progress."

"Thank you. Don't worry," I said, "I'll take them home."

I put David in the back seat, drove him home, and never said a word. When we got home, I said, "What happened?"

"We just got into the shampoo."

"That's OK. We did dumber things than that when we were young. Go to bed now."

Two days later, the country club phoned us up and kicked us out. They canceled our membership because of our juvenile delinquent. I went to David and said, "David, you got us kicked out of the country club." His eyes lit up. I said, "But it's OK, don't worry; it doesn't matter." He was clear that he was safe.

Recently David and I were talking. He said, "I remember the country club. I remember when you came and picked me up. You took me home, and you never said a word. You backed me 100 percent. I still remember that. You did that with all of us; it was the greatest thing in the world."

Constant positive reinforcement is one of the most wonderful things you can do. Positively reinforce yourself as well.

Whatever Is Expressed Is Impressed

Another law says that *whatever is expressed is impressed*. Whenever you say anything that raises the self-esteem and self-confidence of another person, you automatically raise your own. By making another person feel happy and positive, you feel happy and positive.

If you are going to take a first-aid course, when do you take it? At the scene of the accident, when somebody is bleeding, or before? Obviously you want to take it before, so that you're fully prepared.

It's exactly the same thing with positive self-talk and reversals and setbacks in life. Talk to yourself on a positive basis all the time, so that when you experience unexpected reversals and failures, you are subconsciously prepared to be resilient, like the bamboo tree. You will take the initial shock, and you will bounce back immediately.

Talk to yourself. Say these magic words: *I can do it. I can do it. I can do it*. If somebody else is doubtful, say, *you can do it*. Many people's lives have been changed by one person saying, *you can do it*.

Whenever I come across anyone who is doing a good job, say a waitress or hotel employee, I say, "You've got star quality, and you're going to be a big success." I may never see them again, but I know that many people's lives have been changed forever because one person took the time to tell them that they were good and that they had great potential. After all the negative messages in their lives, they grab your message and hold on to it.

I've had people come up to me and say, "You may not remember, but I was in jail and you wrote to me," or "I met you at a seminar in Kansas City, and my life was in shambles. Now this is my life today, and it's wonderful. I have my own business, a beautiful home, and family. You changed my life. You took the time to talk to me, you wrote to me, you called me, you sent me a message. I still have it, I still look at it, I have it on my desk, because nobody had ever told me that."

This law of reversibility says that the more you tell other people how good they are, the more you say the same things to yourself. Also, the more you talk to yourself in a positive way, the more naturally you talk to other people in a positive way.

Autosuggestion

There is a process for getting into the habit of daily positive self-talk. Napoleon Hill called it *autosuggestion*, or self-suggestion. Today we call it *autoconditioning*: we are conditioned by ourselves.

There are two types of conditioning. One is autoconditioning, where you condition yourself by talking to yourself. Then there's *heteroconditioning*, which means being conditioned by others by having them talk to us and influence us. The best, of course, is to have both, but at least you can control autosuggestion.

There's a five-step process for learning how to talk to yourself in a positive way.

1. IDEALIZE

Idealize. This means that you project yourself forward and imagine that your life is perfect in every way. If your life were perfect in every way, what would it look like? What would you be doing? How would you feel? What would you be accomplishing?

I teach this to corporations who are going through strategic planning exercises. I'll have everyone in the room imagine that this company is perfect in five years. If it were perfect in five years, how would people describe it from the outside? If a major magazine were doing a story on this company, what would you want them to say?

People respond by saying things like, "This is the best company in its industry. It has the highest-quality products, great customer service, tremendous technology, regular growth rates, the best leadership, the best training, the best people, and a stock value three times as high as it was five years before." (These, by the way, turn out to be the characteristics of all the best companies.)

I say, "All right, now, are these ideals possible?"

They stop and say, "Yes. Not in one year, but in three years or five years, we could accomplish all of those."

I walked a company through this process a few years ago. They came up with seventeen ideal descriptions, almost like affir-

---

**If your life were perfect in every way, what would it look like?
What would you be doing? How would you feel?
What would you be accomplishing?**

---

mations of what the company would look like if it were perfect in five years. At that time, they were at $20 million in sales. One of their goals was to be at $40 million, with double the sales and of course double the profitability.

They began to initiate all of these ideas enthusiastically; everyone got into it. Five years later, they called me and invited me to a special dinner in downtown Washington at the Ritz Carlton: "We'd like you to come; we're celebrating our five-year anniversary of that strategic planning session." They paid my way, so I went.

It was beautiful. They had a live jazz orchestra, with fabulous food. Then they announced that this year they had hit $104 million in sales—five years after they had set a goal to hit $40 million. They exceeded their goal by 500 percent, and they said it was all because of that exercise in idealizing.

The first thing you do to exceed your goals is to create an exciting future picture of what your business and life would look like in the future if they were perfect in every way.

2. VISUALIZE

The second thing you do is *visualize*. You imagine; you create a mental picture of that success. Remember, you cannot accomplish something on the outside unless you can visualize it on the inside.

One couple went through a seminar explaining this process. They said they wanted to have a dream house. I said, "Then get some pictures of dream houses. Buy some beautiful magazines that are full of pictures, like *House Beautiful, Architectural Digest,* and *Better Homes and Gardens.*"

They went out and did that. Two years passed. They called me up and said, "You're not going to believe what happened after

---

**You cannot accomplish something on the outside
that you cannot visualize on the inside.**

---

that seminar. We went out, and we idealized. We found these magazines and we subscribed to them, and we started to tear out pictures of rooms and gardens so that we could create our perfect composite home.

"Then we made a big file folder with all these pictures. We would take it out, and we'd look at it every week. We'd think about and dream about living in that home. Then, a year later, we got an announcement that my husband was being transferred out west." In this case, it was to Edmonton, Alberta.

The first thing the husband had to do was buy a house. He went out on a Tuesday or Wednesday. He called up a couple of real estate agents, and he remembered the picture that he had. He said, "We're looking for a house that has these aspects and this view and this number of rooms."

The listing agent said, "I know everything in the inventory in town. There is no house like that for sale right now, but there is a house just like that coming on the list tomorrow. You could be one of the first people to see it."

His wife came out on Friday, and on Saturday morning the real estate agent picked them up from the hotel. They drove out to this house, and they walked in. It was the perfect house from *Better Homes and Gardens*—the one that they had been dreaming about and visualizing for two years. The price was right; the location was right. They bought the house, and they're living in it today. They said, "It was like a dream; it was the house we had dreamed of."

There are five aspects to visualization:

- *Clarity.* The clearer the mental picture of the person you want to be, or the things you want to have, the faster they come into reality. It's almost like a one-to-one relationship: clarity and realization.
- *Vividness.* How vivid is the picture that you see?
- *Intensity.* How excited are you about achieving this goal?
- *Duration.* How long can you hold this visual picture in your mind before being distracted?
- *Repetition.* How often each day do you create this mental picture?

3. VERBALIZE

Step number three is to *verbalize.* Remember, your mind is activated by powerful words; this is where you create an affirmation. You can say, "I live in a beautiful 5,000-square-foot home overlooking the river, in a lovely neighborhood, where my children can go to excellent schools."

That's a good verbalization. It's maybe a bit long, but now you have a clear picture. If you're not specific in your verbalization, there may be a house for sale, but it might not have a view. There's a house for sale, but it might not be in a good neighborhood. There's a house for sale, but it's too small or too large.

The universe wants you to be crystal clear about what you want. It's like planting a seed in a very rich soil. The universe, nature, will grow the seed. Your job is to plant it and keep it clear: keep the weeds away. Nature will just grow it naturally.

If you don't plant flowers in a garden, what will grow? Weeds. Weeds—negative thinking—grow automatically. With flowers, vegetables—positive thinking—you have to weed them. Verbalize and create a clear verbal statement of your goal.

For many years, I got three by five index cards, and I would write my affirmations: *I achieve this goal by this date. I weigh this amount. I swim this far. I drive this type of a car. I live in this type of a home. I earn this amount of money.* I never wrote anything on those cards that I didn't eventually achieve: be a best-selling author, travel around the world, earn a certain amount of money, live in a beautiful home, have lovely children. I wrote everything down and reread it over and over.

One of the most powerful forms of affirmation is written affirmation. Write down your positive statements in words, then reread them and recite them to yourself every day.

I would also review my affirmations morning and night. You can work on as many as fifteen goals at a time this way. Every morning, I would sit and read the goal, and I would create a picture of this goal as already achieved.

Emotionalize your picture. Think how you would feel if you achieved this goal—proud, happy, excited, warm, thrilled, secure. Combine the emotion with the verbalization: *I earn this amount of money by this date.* If I earn this amount of money, how will I feel? What will I do, what will I look like, what will be different in my life? Make that affirmation come to life. It's got to be vivid, exciting, clear, emotional, and intense. It's got to be written down so that you can trigger the picture and the emotion every time you read it. I would read my affirmation twice

---

**Write down your positive statements in words,
then reread and recite them to yourself every day.**

---

a day and take a few seconds to visualize the goal as already realized.

4. ACTUALIZE

The next step is to *actualize*—in other words, take the actions consistent with achieving the goal. Act as if the goal is guaranteed, and do the actions that come to your mind and lie clearly at hand. Get up each morning, go to work, do the very best job you can, and have absolute trust that the goal is moving towards you in the most remarkable ways.

5. REALIZATION

The final principle is *realization*. At exactly the right time for you, in exactly the right way, the goal will appear. It will appear not too soon and not too late; you can never push to have the goal appear. The goal will appear exactly when you are ready for it, so just be patient and completely trusting, as though an extremely wealthy man of high integrity had absolutely guaranteed that he was going to deliver this goal to you at exactly the moment that was best for you. Just relax, as though it's money in the bank.

This relaxation creates the catalyst. It's almost like the chemical substance within which the goal is realized. The more relaxed you are, the more calm you are, the more rapidly the goal materializes in your life.

These are the things that you need to do, and if you do them, you'll find your whole life starts to dance. You're more positive, you have more energy, and things start to happen around you to move you towards your goal.

Empowering Questions

We are also constantly asking questions of ourselves. We're either asking positive questions like, *how can I do this?* and *how can I solve this?* or negative things like, *why does this always happen to me? Why can I never follow through?* Again, it seems that the negative approach is the most common: *Why does that always happen to me? Why can't I afford what I need?*

Top people think most of the time about what they want and how to get it. The most important question in continuous motivation is to think about what you want and about what actions you can take now to move you closer to the goal: *how can I achieve this goal?* Every time you ask the question *how*, you trigger action ideas—things that you can do immediately. Napoleon Hill said, "The only real cure for worry is continuous action in the direction of your goals, because you get so busy working towards your goals that you have no time to think negatively at all."

Never say anything that you don't want to be true about yourself. Don't say, "I always mess up," or "Why do I make mistakes like this?" Always say, "What can I learn from this that will make me smarter next time?" Your mind can only hold one thought at a time. If you ask this question, and you focus on your lessons, you don't have time to be negative, because looking for a positive lesson makes you a positive person.

You will always find at least one, and sometimes several, lessons that you can learn from any setback or difficulty. Practically all wealthy people have made an enormous number of mistakes on the way to wealth, and have learned from each one. When unsuccessful people make a mistake, they blame it on others. When successful people make a mistake, they look upon it as a gift from

God: "There's something in this that can help me to make sure that I am fully prepared for my success." As Earl Nightingale said, "If you achieve your success and you're not ready for it, you'll just feel foolish, and you'll lose it quite quickly." Easy come, easy go.

The way to hold on to your success is to learn from every experience. Ask, "What did I do right, and what would I do differently if I had to do this over?" What you would do differently contains the lessons. You can stomp on the accelerator of your self-growth by constantly reviewing your performance in a positive way.

If you achieve your success and you're not ready for it, you'll just feel foolish, and you'll lose it quite quickly.

Teach What You Want to Learn

When you teach something to other people, you instill it in yourself at a deeper level. You become what you teach. If we have a compulsion to teach, it's because we want to learn the subject ourselves at a deeper level.

In order to teach something, you have to go into the subject in depth. You have to look at it from many different sides. Once you have fully learned the subject, you lose interest in teaching it. You'll want to teach other things.

I teach business model reinvention. I put in 300 hours of studying over two years. I read the best books and articles on the subject, took notebooks full of notes, and reviewed the notes. I put workbooks together and taught the subject. Then I revised the workbooks, taught it again, and revised and revised. Now I'm able to apply these ideas to my own business. My income has gone up, as has my life satisfaction.

Many years ago, I took a course in accelerated learning. One part is called *dual-plane learning.* First, learn the material yourself, but as you're learning it, think about teaching it. This way, you're taking in the information on two levels, which doubles and triples the amount that you learn and retain. You're much more likely to internalize the information if you think, "How could I teach this? To whom would I teach this? To whom would this be of value? What if I were going to write an article on this?"

When you're thinking about your subject like this, you learn at a much more rapid rate. When you start to actually teach it to people, your learning goes up five or ten times.

Self-Talk for Kids

This idea of self-talk is critical for a parent raising kids. If they start young, they're going to be way ahead of the game. When your children doubt themselves, tell them, "You did a great job; you did the best you possibly could. You'll do better next time; there's always a next time." Tell them how excellent they are.

Let's go back to this simple statement: *I like myself.* A woman once said she had heard that from me, and she struggled with it because of her negative upbringing. She didn't like herself; she didn't think she was that good; she felt inferior. Suddenly she had a breakthrough, and she started saying to herself, *I love myself. I love myself.* She said that all she had wanted as a child was for her parents to love her. Since they didn't, someone had to love her, and it had to be herself.

One interesting study says that our self-esteem is largely created by the distance between our self-image, the way we see ourselves today, and where we dream of being in the future. It's also determined by where we are today relative to our expectations. Where did we expect to be at this stage of our life, and are we at that stage?

A great deal of depression, alcoholism, and other negative behavior occurs among people who have expected to be at a certain point at a certain stage in life, and they're not. They expected, for example, to have more money and more success. This gap between where they are and where they expected to be causes them enormous stress. Sometimes they even kill themselves.

The highest rate of suicide in America is in males between the ages of forty-eight and fifty-two. That's the point where they realize, *I'm never going to make it.* They had high expectations for themselves, going back to their parents. Their parents always demanded that they excel.

I remember a story about a boy who comes home with average grades. His father beats him up, saying, "Why are you getting such lousy grades? What's the matter? Are you stupid or something?"

The kid decides to work hard and get good grades. He cancels his social activities. He comes home and studies for four or five hours a night for the entire semester. He takes six courses. He gets five A's and one B, and he comes home and shows his report card to his father. The father glances at it and says, "Why did you get a B?" That takes away all his desire to excel: he never tries in school again. His father has destroyed his motivation.

The most wonderful thing you can do is always tell your kids how good they are: "Hey, you did great, and you'll do better next time." Never be disappointed in your kids. Never say, "If you'd only done this . . ." or, "If you had only done that differently."

It's like that story of my son with the shampoo in the Jacuzzi. I said, "That's OK. I made mistakes when I was young." That's a formative event: decades later, he still remembers. He remembers how concerned he was with how I would respond to the police, and I just laughed. We've done that with every problem our kids have gotten into. All good kids get into things like that; we just laugh.

To come back full circle, you become what you say to yourself most of the time. You have total control over what you say to yourself. Deliberately talk to yourself in a positive way. Never say anything about yourself that you don't want to be true.

Never say, "I look overweight." Say, "My ideal weight is such and such, by such and such a date." Or "I weigh this number of pounds by this date." Always think about the future. Forget about the past, which you can't change. Always create affirmations for your wonderful, exciting future, and they will come true just as surely as seeds bloom in summertime.

A Review of the 5 Steps for Positive Self-Talk

1. *Idealize*—project yourself forward and imagine your life is perfect.
2. *Visualize*—create a mental picture of your success.
3. *Verbalize*—activate your mind with powerful words.
4. *Actualize*—take the actions consistent with achieving the goal.
5. *Realization*—The goal will appear exactly when you are ready for it.

SEVEN

Thinking in the Long Term

The natural tendency of human beings is to look for the fastest and easiest way to get the things they want right now, with very little concern over the long-term consequences. I call this the *expediency factor* or the *E-factor*.

At Harvard University in the fifties, Dr. Edward Banfield completed a series of studies looking for the reasons for upward socioeconomic mobility—in other words, increasing income over time. He studied both nationally and internationally to find out why some people move up more rapidly in the income ladder.

He found that across all socioeconomic levels, there is only one quality that predicted rapid upper socioeconomic mobility: long-term perspective. Long-time perspective meant that the individual spent a lot of time thinking in the long term—five, ten,

---

The E-Factor (Expediency Factor): The tendency for human beings to look for the fastest and easiest way to get the things they want now, with little concern for long-term consequences.

---

and even twenty years out into the future when planning their current activities. A book called *Competing for the Future*, which was published in the nineties, argued that long-term perspective dramatically improved short-term decision making.

One key to success is to think in terms of where you want to be in the future—psychologically, financially, economically, socially—come back to the present, and ask, "What do I have to do today to be sure that I achieve those goals in the long term?" This requires planning, thinking, sacrifice, hard work, and delayed gratification.

The simplest way to become wealthy is to work hard, save your money, and let it grow by compounding. Back in 1980, there were something like one million self-made millionaires. In 2016 there were ten million self-made millionaires, and the number's growing by several hundred thousand each year.

Why? If at age twenty-five you were to save $100 a month, $25 a week, out of your income, invest it carefully in a good mutual fund, and let it grow with the rate of the economy, by the time you retired forty-five years later, with compounding you'd be more than a millionaire. That's long-term perspective.

I've met farmers, crane operators, doormen, taxi drivers, and laborers who became millionaires over the course of their working lives. The families living on either side of them were spending everything they earned and a little bit more, while these people were saving between 10 and 20 percent of their income and tightening their belt a little. They went out for dinner a little bit less and shopped at discount stores. They were looking for ways to cut corners. Then they put the money away and never touched it.

Long-term perspective turns out to be the single most important quality for success. You could give a high salary to every single person in every single neighborhood in America, but if they didn't have long-term perspective, they'd soon blow through all the money.

There is the 80/20 rule: the top 20 percent of people in a society have 80 percent of the wealth. You could take all the wealth of a society and divide it up equally. Within one year, the top 20 percent would have 80 percent of the money, because the top 20 percent are always looking for ways to create the future: to save, invest, and so on. The bottom 80 percent would just go out and blow it.

So ask yourself, what are your goals in ten or twenty years? Then ask yourself every minute of every day, "Is what I'm doing right now moving me toward my most important goals or not?"

Here's a simple technique for doubling your productivity: divide your everyday tasks into A tasks and B tasks. A tasks and activities move you toward your goals B tasks do *not* move you toward your goals, or, even worse, move you away from them.

To double your productivity, to become rich, healthy, successful, and highly respected, simply be crystal clear about your goals, and then do only A tasks all day long. Do not do B tasks at all. That alone will supercharge your productivity. It'll make you the go-to person in your field. It'll move you into the top 10 percent.

Just do A activities—the ones that have long-term consequences, that contribute to achieving the most important things in life.

The Marshmallow Test

The marshmallow test was a great study done at Harvard some years ago. The psychologist put a bunch of children, ages six to eight, in a room around a table, and said, "Here is a marshmallow. We'll leave you here for half an hour. If you can refrain from eating this marshmallow for those thirty minutes, you'll get two marshmallows." Then the researchers went out of the room and watched what the kids did through a one-way mirror.

Some kids sat and stared at the marshmallow; others put their hands over their eyes and looked away from it. Other kids put their arms under their shoulders to hold themselves back from touching the marshmallow. Still other kids picked up the marshmallow, put it down, and nibbled at it. They ate a little bit more and finally consumed the whole thing.

Ten years later, the psychologists found that when these children were in their teens, the ones that had resisted eating the marshmallow were getting better grades. As they went into their twenties, they became high achievers. Even twenty years later, they were earning more money and were in higher positions.

As for the kids who had consumed the marshmallow immediately, nothing ever came of them. They got poor grades, they were not particularly successful or popular, and ten or twenty years later they were working at average jobs.

What caused the difference? The kids who did not eat the marshmallows were brought up by their parents to feel confident and secure in themselves. The reason people eat a lot of food goes back to prehistory. In the wintertime, there would be no food, so you would eat a lot beforehand, like a bear that's going to hibernate. You'd eat and fatten up, because the lean months were coming.

Today if an insecure person gets a chance to eat some food or enjoy immediate gratification, they grab it, because in the back of their mind, they're not sure if they're going to get more in the future. That's why in dieting, if you starve yourself, you put on an enormous amount of weight when you start to eat again. The mind has this idea registered: "Gee, I'd better load up here."

When many overweight people go on a diet, they think, "As soon as I lose five pounds, I can go out and gorge myself." Their reward for losing weight is to gorge. But if they starve themselves, their body says, *red alert, red alert.* It drives them to think about nothing but going out and gorging themselves.

On the other hand, if you are secure because your parents made you feel like a valuable and important person, totally secure in their love—we call this unconditional love—you will be able to defer gratification in favor of later rewards. It's not genetic. It's upbringing.

Kids who passed the marshmallow tests were more successful in their teens and twenties because they grew up with high self-confidence and high self-esteem. When you have high self-esteem, you set bigger goals for yourself. You persist longer, and you become unstoppable.

Even if you weren't raised that way, psychology has developed some powerful techniques to teach people to delay gratification. Goethe said, "Everything is hard before it is easy."

"Everything is hard before it is easy."
—Goethe, poet and playwright

Self-Discipline and Self-Esteem

It's important to develop good habits. This requires self-discipline, which in turn is closely tied to self-esteem. Self-discipline is the single most important quality for success. If you discipline yourself to hold off gratification and complete a task before you give yourself a reward, it will raise your self-esteem and self-confidence. It improves your character and makes you stronger. Moreover, every act of self-discipline strengthens every subsequent act of self-discipline.

One thing you can do is set up a reward system for task completion. In sales, there is a direct relationship between dials and dollars—how many times you pick up the phone and dial. However, the fear of rejection holds people back.

A friend of mine developed a very simple technique. He would take a steaming hot cup of coffee, and he'd put it in front of him. He would not allow himself a sip of the coffee until he had contacted a prospect. He sat down with the phone, made the call, and talked to the prospect. When he hung up, he gave himself a sip of coffee.

But the coffee was getting cold, so he'd make another call as quickly as he could. He didn't care too much about whether or not the customer was interested; he was concerned about getting to the next sip before the coffee got cold. Each time he got through to somebody, he'd give himself a sip of coffee. By the time he got to the fifth person, the coffee cup was empty. This is a form of inverted psychology, whereby you take your focus off the task and put it onto something different to diminish the stress.

My friend came up with another idea. He liked cookies, so he would take a cookie and cut it into tiny pieces. He would give himself one little piece of cookie every time he made a call, in the way you would reward an animal for performing an act.

His friends joked with him about it, but within three months, he was the highest-earning salesman in this company. He was breaking every record.

With this approach, your mind starts to think more and more about the reward and less and less about the tension of making the call and being rejected.

So this is one thing you can do: set up a reward structure for engaging in good behavior. If you're doing a big job, divide it into small pieces, and give yourself a little reward for the completion of each small piece.

Maybe the first reward is a piece of cookie. Maybe you say that if you do ten calls, you stand up, stretch, and walk around. Maybe if you make twenty calls, you check your email for the first time in the day.

Checking emails is a dessert activity; it's not a dinner activity, and the key to success is to have dinner before dessert. If you come in in the morning and check email, you're eating your dessert first. It's as if you sat down at dinner and had a big piece of apple pie and ice cream right away. How much appetite would you have for the main course?

When people start off with dessert in the workplace, for the rest of the day they waste time. They want more dessert. They send out more messages. They check their email continually. They read the paper. They bother other people. They can't get into work, because they've had dessert.

When you get an email, it's very much like a slot machine: you pull the lever, and it rings. You don't know what's going to happen. Are you going to win? Are you going to lose? You anticipate the surprise. It's a shiny-object mentality. When your email announcement goes off—*Bing! You have email*—it immediately stops you from what you're doing. You say, "Oh, I wonder what I won. Maybe it's a friend; maybe it's a joke."

Wasting Time at Work

Today an average of 50 percent of work time is wasted in non-work activities. Many people beat the average. Highly productive people are way below the average in this respect.

If you ask people whether they waste time at work, they'll say, "Absolutely not. I go in and hit it all day." But if you placed a hidden camera to watch these people, this is what you would find: The person comes to work. The first thing they do is greet their coworkers as if they haven't seen them for six months. Like hummingbirds going from flower to flower, they go from person to person, reestablishing their relationship. *How are you doing? How is everything going? What did you do last night? What did you see on television? Oh, that looks nice. Where did you get that?* Finally the person realizes they had better get some work done before the boss comes by.

The average person today does not start work until 11:00 a.m. Then, at about a quarter to twelve, they start to wind down for lunch. They have a sixty-minute lunch, but they take ninety minutes. They come back at 1:30, and they have to reestablish all their friendships in the office. They haven't seen these people for ninety minutes, so again they go around like a hummingbird from person to person. Finally they realize, "Gee, I had better get some work done," so at about 2:30 or 3:00, they do a little bit of work. Then they start to wind down at 3:30.

Rush hour traffic in Los Angeles starts at 3:30. The 401, one of the major freeways, turns into a parking lot. If you get onto the freeway after 3:30, you're going to be there for hours. What would otherwise take you sixty minutes will take you five to six hours.

**Today an average of 50% of work time
is wasted in non-work activities.**

Who are all the people on the freeway at this time? They're people who don't get off until 5:00. They're trying to beat the traffic home by getting onto the freeway by 3:30.

If you ask people whether they waste time, they will say, "No, no." It's called *invisible time wastage.* When you play back the recording with a meter showing the minutes and seconds, people are shocked. They had no idea that they were wasting most of their time.

By wasting so much time, you're destroying your hopes and dreams for the future. It's because you don't have a long-term perspective.

Start your day with a very clear schedule, planned and structured. Set priorities on that schedule, and then put your head down and hit it hard all day long. When you walk in, wave—hi, everybody!—and go straight to work. *Work all the time you work.* If someone says, "Hey, have you got a minute to talk right now?" say, "I'd love to. Let's talk after work. I have to get back to work."

Back to work. Back to work. Whenever you find yourself drifting, keep saying, *back to work, back to work.* Pretty soon people will leave you alone. They'll find that you're not interesting; you're not ready to hang around for indefinite periods of time.

Walk in, say hello, and go straight to work. Put your head down, and work all the time you work. When you've finished your work, you can raise your head and chat with people. Let them ruin their careers, but don't let them ruin yours.

The most powerful tool you have is your ability to think and especially your ability to think *in advance*. It's thinking about the consequences of your behaviors: if I do this, what is likely to happen? In fact, the ability to accurately predict the consequences of your behavior before you act is the highest mark of intelligence. The person who can play down the chessboard of life and calculate, "If I do this, life will do that; then I will do this; I'll have to do that." All successful people play several steps ahead.

Distraction and Multitasking

There are two major obstacles to proper brain functioning today. Number one is *distraction*. We are distracted by so many things, especially electronic distractions.

The second is *multitasking*, where you're trying to do several things at once. Books and articles have written on the myth of multitasking. It *is* a myth, because we don't multitask. Instead we shift from task to task. We're focused like a light beam on one task; then we get a bing, and we switch to the computer to check the email. Then we switch back, but it takes between seven and seventeen minutes to get back to the task.

Success does not come from *working on* tasks. It comes from *completing* tasks. Eighty-two percent of Americans would like to write a book. They would like to be published authors; they would like to tell their stories. Some of them even take a run at it. But they never complete it. The world is full of incomplete manuscripts, incomplete poems, incomplete business plans. It's task completion that's the key to success.

Here's a tremendous way to promote a long-term perspective. When you start off in the morning, make a list of everything you

---

The Two Major Obstacles to Proper Brain Functioning:
1. Distraction
2. Multitasking

---

have to do that day. Never start work without a list. The best thing is to make the list the night before. If something new comes up, write it on the list before you do it. Don't get thrown off track by a shiny object—somebody calling you, texting you, or anything else. Write it down before you do it.

When you start work, you're planned and prepared. You look at your task list and say, "If I could only do one job on this list before I was called out of town for a month, which one would it be?" You start work on that; you put your head down and work nonstop for ninety minutes. You turn off your television, your phone, your computer. Put your head down and work nonstop for ninety minutes.

Then get up, give yourself a break, walk around, and get a cup of coffee or tea, for fifteen minutes. Then come back and sit down and go back to your task again for another ninety minutes. Then check your email. You've now had dinner. Your email is your dessert.

If you can do two flat-out ninety-minute work sessions without interruption or distraction every morning, you will double, triple, and quadruple your productivity, and eventually your income. You will complete more and more tasks. You'll become known as the go-to person.

Many years ago, I was struggling and working my way up. I put together a real estate deal, and I managed to tie up the property. But I didn't have any money. So I began visiting development companies, and I finally stumbled across one. They said, "If your numbers hold up, we'd be interested in coming in with you as a partner."

I had read all the books on real estate development. I knew exactly how to put together a pro forma. I put together this proposal. I sat down with their real estate development lawyers. I showed them corroboration for every single number and statement in the account. I had letters of intent from major tenants. I had letters of cost analysis from a construction company. I listed every single cost and every single source of revenue.

At the end the lawyers said, "This is the most complete business proposal we've ever seen." They checked it out and said, "OK, we'll come in. We'll pay 100 percent of all the costs of developing this shopping center for 75 percent ownership, leaving you 25 percent to carry it through to completion." They did, and I did.

Not long after that, the president of this company, one of the richest and most respected men in Canada, called me into his office. He said, "I like your work ethic. You fulfilled every promise that you ever made on schedule. How would you like to come and work for me as my personal assistant?"

So I went to work for him. He would give me little assignments to do, almost like a mentee. He'd never had a personal assistant before, so I had to ask him, "I need something to do," and he would give it to me.

Whatever it was, I'd run out and do it immediately and bring it back. He didn't say very much, but he would nod and smile. A few days later, he'd give me something else to do. These were little things, but whatever he gave me to do, I ran out, did it, and came back immediately. He said, "Boy, that was fast. You really take this seriously. It's not that important. Next week would have been fine."

Then a big opportunity came up, and he said, "Do you want to take a look at this?" It turned into a $25 million importation and distribution company, and he made me the president.

Another opportunity came up. It was a major real estate development: several hundred acres, homes, industrial parks, commercial, residential. "Would you like to take a look at this?" my boss asked. I put a plan together and brought it back to him, so he put me in charge of this new development. Then he said, "We're planning on building a downtown office building. We're not exactly sure how it should be configured, what the cost should be, what the rents will be. Would you like to take a look at that?" Pretty soon I was in charge of developing a twelve-story office building in the center of downtown.

My boss kept giving me assignments. Every time he did, I would jump and do them immediately. I was working ten or twelve hours a day, and I worked all the time I worked.

By the end of my time with my boss—when he retired—I was running three major divisions of the company. I was making more money than I'd ever dreamed of in my life. I had received more experience than I ever expected. I had a staff of forty-two work-ing in my three divisions. I had the biggest office in the company next to his. I was beyond everyone else who worked in this large conglomerate.

When they gave me a task, I did it, I did it fast, and I did it 100 percent. If you wanted something done in a month or two, you would give it to one of the other people. If you wanted it done now and you wanted it done quickly and well, you would give it to Brian. "Whatever you give to Brian, no matter how busy he is, he'll get it done." That's the way you develop a long-term perspective. I realized that I wasn't working just for the short term; I was working to develop myself and my abilities for the long term.

After I left this gentleman, we remained friends forever, and I was ten years further along in my career than I could ever have dreamed possible. I had more experience and knowledge, and I was able to earn more money. I went on to develop $100 million worth of real estate with the skills that I had learned under his supervision and tutelage.

The long-term perspective means you work hard in the short term and work every single day, putting in two ninety-minute sessions every morning. You work all the time you work. Give yourself rewards and gratification. "After I put in three solid hours, I'll check my email, because email is dessert. Then I'll take myself out for lunch. I deserve lunch now because I've done this work."

When you come back, hit your work again. Develop a reputation for being the hardest-working person in your organization. If they brought in an outside firm of management consultants who asked everybody in the office, "Who is the hardest worker here?" be sure that you would win. Nothing will move you ahead faster than to be known as the hardest-working, most productive person in your business.

Develop a reputation for being the hardest-working person in your organization.

Feeling Like a Winner

Everybody wants to feel like a winner. If you do, you have high self-esteem. The more you win, the more confidence you have, the happier you are, the more respected you are. How do you get the winning feeling? You win. You cross the finish line.

In work, you set up the job, and you break it down into smaller pieces. Let me give you an example.

Many companies used to reward their salespeople when they made the sale, but if the sale was, say, a large piece of equipment, the process could take five to seven months. That was the cycle from the time you contacted the prospect and went through the bidding. submission, design, and installation process. Then the salesperson would get the reward.

This was obviously damaging the salespeople's motivation, because they weren't getting any immediate payoff for all the work they were doing. So the companies divided this sales process into seven parts. The first part was coming face-to-face and identifying a real-life prospect who wanted, needed, and could pay for the product. That was a source of celebration, and the company would give hands of applause for having opened the door, cracked the ice, and started the process.

The next step would be the submission of an initial bid based on an analysis of the client's situation. The salesperson would get rewards based on that. In short, every time they completed a step, they were made to feel like a winner.

Motivating Children

We found the same thing with our children. With every single thing that our children have ever started and completed, whether it's cleaning up their room, painting a picture in kindergarten, or reading a book, we make a big thing of it. Wow! Holy smokes!

If you do that, eventually your children will strive for opportunities to win. They will become impatient with playing online, with being "screenagers." They will want to get good grades. They will want to do things that make them feel like winners, because their parents have always made them feel like winners when they completed a task.

In the Bible it says, "O good and faithful servant, you have been faithful over small things. I will make you master over many." If you praise and encourage your children when they do little things, they will do bigger and bigger things, and they'll be much more easily detached from their friends who are doing useless stuff. They'll say, "I have to go home now. I have to get my assignment done." You don't even have to threaten or demand. They'll feel so good that they'll get good grades all by themselves.

Incidentally, the way to become the most important influence in your child's life is to become the most important source of emotional support and unconditional love. Your child will be influenced by their peers and friends, but your child always has to know that you are the most important person in their life because you are totally dedicated to them.

"O good and faithful servant, you have been faithful over small things. I will make you master over many." —The Bible

---

Management by Quadrants

The quadrant theory of time management breaks everything you do into four parts. Imagine a box divided in half and half again, so there are four squares. You number the squares: 1, the upper left-hand square; 2, the upper right-hand square; 3, the lower left-hand square; and 4, the lower right-hand square. Now you have four quadrants. Then you divide them up again based on urgency and importance. The degree of importance runs down the left side, so quadrant number 1 is both important and urgent. This is quadrant 1. It's on the upper left. It's called the *quadrant of immediacy.* This is almost always determined by external forces—commitments, things that you have to do and you have to get done *now*: meetings you have to go to, customers you have to call, and so on.

By the way, if you don't do these things, they can be very dangerous for your job. If you don't get that assignment done, if you don't bring in those sales, if you don't complete a particular task, you could lose your job, so this is where you start. You always work in the quadrant of immediacy.

Now the quadrant in the upper right is quadrant number 2. It's the quadrant of things that are important but not urgent. This is called the *quadrant of effectiveness.* These are the things that have long-term potential consequences in your life: upgrading your skills, taking additional courses, writing out proposals and plans and reports, and reading. Anything that you do that is not urgent but important is in quadrant 2. Everything that's in quadrant 2 can be delayed. You *can* procrastinate about it, but whatever is in quadrant 2 that is not urgent will soon become urgent.

The Quadrant Theory of Time Management

1. Important and urgent: the quadrant of immediacy	2. Important but not urgent: the quadrant of effectiveness
3. Urgent but not important: the quadrant of delusion	4. Neither urgent nor important: the quadrant of waste

A perfect example is in college. They will tell you at the beginning of the course that 50 percent of your final grade will be determined by your final paper. You must submit this paper by 8:00 in the morning on this date, or you will lose 50 percent of your credit for this course.

The instructor will repeat this every week: "Remember, 50 percent of your grade will depend on your final paper. Do not delay. Do not procrastinate. Begin working on it now. Get it done early."

What happens? Ninety percent of students put the paper off because it's not urgent yet. It's very important; it determines their whole success in this course, which may even amount to their whole success in the year. But they put it off.

When are most final papers written? The night before. I did this when I was taking an MBA degree. I'd come home at 5:00 p.m. I'd make a big pot of coffee, sit down at my little kitchen table, and begin writing. I'd write all night, and I'd just keep pouring the coffee. As the sun came up, I'd get in my car, race over to the professor's office, and slip the final paper under his door. When I looked under his door, I saw it was jammed with final papers. Everybody did them at the last minute. For a long time the paper was important, but it wasn't urgent. But at a certain point it became extremely urgent—more urgent than anything else.

Get everything done in quadrant 1: the things you have to do now. Then start doing things in quadrant 2, which have long-term potential consequences.

Quadrant 3, on the lower left, includes activities that are urgent but not important. These are people talking to you, emails, somebody coming to your desk, chatting with people, going for lunch, and so on. These are urgent because they're right in your

---

If you want to transform your career, your business and your personal life, spend the majority of your time in Quadrant 2.

---

face, but they're not important. This is called the *quadrant of delusion*. You're at work, and you're interacting with people, so you delude yourself into thinking, *I'm actually working. This is part of my employment. This is what I need to do to get along with my coworkers. I need to have fun at work.*

Anybody who tells you that you need to have fun at work is a loser. This person will retire poor, will have to live on pensions, and will probably go to a senior citizens' home, where nobody will visit them.

It's not that you don't enjoy or laugh with your coworkers, but you do it in the context of working together to get the job done, not just sitting around shooting the breeze. In the quadrant of delusion, people delude themselves into thinking they are working when what they're doing is totally useless.

The fourth quadrant, on the lower right, is the quadrant where it's neither urgent nor important, and this is called the *quadrant of waste*: reading the newspaper, checking through random emails, looking for what's for sale, calling home to see what's for dinner.

Your job is to switch everything over. Spend all of your time in quadrants 1 and 2. Get everything done that must be done as quickly as possible—that's both important and urgent—and then spend more and more time in quadrant 2. Those activities have long-time value and can make a huge difference in your business.

Let me recapitulate the goal setting exercise. Pick your most important goal in life. You can have a goal in your personal life:

your family. You can have a health goal, or a business or career goal. Ask, "What is my biggest and most important business or career goal?"—the one that is going to connect directly to your income, your speed of promotion, your level of respect in the company.

Then ask, "What's the most important activity that I can engage in right now to achieve my most important work goal?" That's where you start at the beginning of the day. You discipline yourself to start there, before you check your email or anything else. You work nonstop on that one task until it's complete, and you do this over and over again until it becomes automatic for you to sit down, start work on your most important task, and work on it full blast until it's complete.

Once you develop the habit of completing your most important task first thing in the morning, you'll become one of the most productive, most respected, and highest-paid people in your field.

EIGHT

The Keys to Resilience

I've already talked about the role of expectations in motivation, attitude, performance, and behavior. Expectations determine your level of resilience, persistence—everything. So we always have to ask, what are your expectations?

Here's an example. Harvard found that leaders hate the idea of losing. They also hate the idea of failing, but they know that it is impossible to achieve anything worthwhile without making mistakes, without losing, without having setbacks and difficulties. So they plunge forward nonetheless.

One thing I have discovered is called *preprogramming*. You can preprogram your subconscious mind well in advance of an incident so that when the inevitable does occur, you're ready. It's like taking a first aid course in advance of the accident.

You can preprogram yourself for the fact that you will have countless mistakes, failures, challenges, obstacles, difficulties, setbacks, and disappointments. These are unavoidable parts of an active life. The only way you *cannot* have these problems is if you sit in a room by yourself. Even then, you could have all kinds of problems.

So you say, "I'm going to have all kinds of problems and difficulties in my life, but I am never going to let them get me down. No matter what happens, I will bounce back. I will find a way through it or around it. I will try again or try something different." Say that to yourself repeatedly.

When you hit an obstacle, a letdown, or a disappointment, you feel as if you've had a punch in the emotional solar plexus. Everybody has a shock of disappointment when something that they expected to go well goes poorly. You feel stunned, knocked back on your heels. But how long do you stay there?

If you have preprogrammed yourself, you automatically bounce back. But if you had an idea that things should be fine and should work out, the clash between expectation and reality makes you depressed and angry.

The critical thing is the gap between expectations and reality. If you expect that life is going to be difficult and you're going to have lots of unexpected setbacks but you're not going to let them get you down, you won't feel depressed when they happen. You automatically bounce back.

Murphy's Law says whatever can go wrong, will go wrong. The first corollary of Murphy's Law is whatever can go wrong will go wrong and will cost the most amount of money. The second corollary is whatever can go wrong, will go wrong, and will take

---

Murphy's Law: Whatever can go wrong, will go wrong, and will 1) cost the most amount of money and 2) take the most amount of time.

---

the most amount of time. Then there's Smith's Law, which said that Murphy was an optimist.

Three and Two

When I work with business owners, I give them the two and three rule: everything that you plan is going to end up costing you twice as much and will take three times as long, or vice versa. This is especially true if you're starting a business and you're looking toward getting to the break-even point. It's going to take you twice as long as your best calculations, and it's going to cost you three times as much money, or vice versa. It's always three and two, or two and three.

People have come back to me and said, "I listened to that, and I said, 'No. That may be true for him or for other people, but not for me.' I knew it wasn't going to apply to me, but it did."

Everything takes twice as long and costs three times as much, or costs three times as much and takes twice as long. So you build that expectation into your calculations. By doing that, when you find that your best expectations don't work out, you're not disappointed or destroyed, because in the back of your mind, you said, "I sort of knew this was going to happen." You can program yourself so that when things do go wrong, you can dance around them like a boxer instead of letting them knock you down.

Look for the good in every situation. If you have a setback or difficulty, say, "That's good." Look into it and ask, "What could be good about this?"

Very often your greatest success is going to come from what appears to be a great failure. Sometimes people will start a business and go bankrupt, but the lessons they learned from that business enable them to be financially successful later. They look and say, "Thank heavens that first business went broke. It was in the wrong industry. Everybody got into that industry and lost everything. We lost, but we lost a small amount in a short period of time. So that was good luck for us. It's almost as if somebody was looking over us to help us to fail." There's a rule that says, *fail fast, learn quickly, try again.*

Once, when I was giving a seminar in Stockholm, four VIPs had paid a special extra fee to have lunch with me during the seminar. They were software engineers.

They were obviously concerned. They said, "We need your advice. You've worked with so many companies."

"All right, what is it?"

"We've been selling this software program, and we found that this business model wasn't working. Sales were difficult. So we created a new business model. The new business model is that we are going to lease the program and service it, so there'll be a much lower upfront initial cost for the client. Not only that, if there are any problems, we'll take care of them, so it's going to be a much easier, cheaper, and ultimately more profitable product, because we'll be able to sell far more of them."

"So what is your problem?" I asked.

"It's not going well. Our revenues are down; our sales force is disagreeing. Customers are used to owning the product. Now they're being told they can't; they can only lease it."

"According to Peter Drucker," I said, "every new business model requires four iterations before you get it right. Sometimes it's much more, but it's a minimum of four. You've only tried one. You have three more different ways of doing it before you get to the average."

You should have seen the smiles of relief that went over their faces. They said, "Thank you so much for telling us that, because we had this expectation that if this was a good, new business model, it should work immediately."

"No, don't worry," I said. "It's like preparing a recipe in the kitchen. No matter how good a cook you are, the first time you prepare a recipe, it's not going to taste that great. So you have to go back and have to change some of the components, ingredients, and proportions. Then go back and taste it—get feedback, and see what happens." As I said earlier, sometimes it takes fourteen times or forty times or 100 times, but you keep working at your model until it works perfectly. Don't expect everything to work perfectly the first time.

Don't expect your great idea to actually be a great idea. Ideas are a dime a dozen; people have hundreds of ideas. Begin by applying what is called *proof of concept.* You say, "I have a great idea for a product or a service or a price or a way that we can market or sell and grow the business."

You go on to say, "Great. That's an idea, but the idea has no value at all. Everybody has ideas; there are millions of them. Now you have to prove that it's true."

How do you prove that it's true? You go to the person you expect to consume your product or service, and you give it to them. You ask them, "Do you like it? Would you buy it? Does it

---

Proof of Concept: Bringing your first iteration of a product or service to a prospective customer and, after as many iterations of the product/service as necessary, proving that the customer would buy it.

---

make you happy? Is this better than our competitors' products? If so, why? If not, why not? What changes do we have to make?"

This is the cutting edge of the future: you begin with the confidence that your first iteration's not going to work, or your second, or your third, or your fourth.

Sales: The Failure Game

When I started off in sales, knocking on doors at age twenty-three, I was selling a small item. It cost $20. It was a membership in a bonus club, where you got a little card. You took it to one of more than 100 restaurants, and you would get a 10 or 20 percent discount on your dinner. It could pay for itself in one use. It was an easy sell. Pay $20, and you could use it indefinitely for a year and save hundreds of dollars. The payoff was tremendous.

Like most young salespeople, I thought everybody would buy this. All I'd have to do was hold it up and tell them what it was, and they'd rip it out of my hand.

I went out and began knocking on doors, and everybody said no. "No, I don't want it. No, I can't afford it. Not in the market right now. I'd probably never go to any of those restaurants." They had every single excuse in the book, and everybody said some version of no.

Finally someone said to me, "This is quite normal. When you start off, you'll get an enormous amount of rejection. In fact, you have to get more rejection. You have to understand that sales is a failure game, not a success game. It's a game of nos. It's a game of probabilities. Your job is to fail more often."

So I used to run between calls. I would run like a runner so I could get rejected more often. I kept doing this until I finally hit on a method of selling, and within one day, my sales tripled. I realized that this is not a sales game; it's a failure game. You're going to fail over and over again in order to be successful. Once you have that attitude, nothing can stop you.

I teach salespeople, "If you want to get your sales career or your company's sales force revved up, have a contest. We call it the 100-call contest. Everybody makes a commitment to go out and make 100 calls as fast as they can without worrying about making sales. A call is actually speaking to a prospect, whether it's on the telephone or face-to-face. For whoever gets to 100 calls first, the company will pay for them and their spouse to go out to the best restaurant in town."

You make it a game, and every day, everybody comes back and reports on the number of calls that they've made. Everybody's racing to be the one that wins the dinner out at the first-class restaurant. Nobody cares if they sell; they just care about getting those numbers. And the sales explode.

Once I was working with a company that did telephone marketing. They put this system in place: they would pay for the lunch of the first person who could get ten nos in the morning.

The salespeople would all line up like horses at the gate, everybody ready with their telephones. At 8:30, someone would say, "Go." Everybody would start dialing and dialing, until finally somebody would jump up and ring the bell. They'd made ten calls and gotten ten rejections faster than anyone else. They'd turn to the other ones and say, "What happened to you?"

"I called somebody, and they wanted to buy, and I had to take the time to take the order and get the money."

"Me too, I made two sales. I just couldn't get to the ten nos because everybody kept wanting to buy."

Every time a company uses this method, they're astonished. First of all, everybody's laughing, so the person on the other end of the phone hears the laugh. The salesperson's positive, smiling, happy. They don't care if you buy; they just want to get through this call. Then the prospect says, "Tell me more about that product. It sounds really good. I was thinking of something like this. How much does it cost? How do I get it?" They begin to sell and sell.

The owner of this company retired as a multimillionaire six years later at the age of fifty. He moved to Palm Springs, and he plays golf every day. He said he never made so much money in his whole life as when nobody cared about rejection.

You're going to fail over and over again in order to be successful. Once you have that attitude, nothing can stop you.

The Crunch Point

You can preprogram yourself to be ready for crisis, but what do you do when crisis hits? Here are some suggestions.

When something goes wrong, stay calm. Just stay calm. Over the years, I've worked with some very wealthy people at times where there are big challenges or crises within their companies; something completely unexpected was going seriously wrong. I would get emotional and upset myself, because I really care for my clients. I watched how they handled it. They would become calm. Every top person I ever met would go dead calm in the middle of a crisis.

Why? You do all of your thinking with your neocortex, the frontal cortex of the brain, which is what makes us uniquely human. This is where we think, analyze, compare, and decide. As long as you are calm, your frontal cortex is on full blast; it's lit up. But as soon as you become angry or emotional, it shuts down. It's like turning off all the lights in a building.

In this case, you revert to your limbic system, which is fight-or-flight. It's stimulated by your emotions: anger, fear, lashing out, blaming. All these negative emotions suddenly dominate your thinking. But as soon as you calm down and take a deep breath, your limbic system, the emotions, settle down. The lobes of your prefrontal cortex open up, and you start to see things with greater clarity.

I've heard about great generals in warfare. Even in the midst of incredible attacks and counterattacks, they become as calm as death. They think and direct the battle calmly and clearly, whereas their enemies get angry and upset and make the wrong decisions, which can be cataclysmic.

The starting point in dealing with a crisis is to stay calm. The next thing is to get the facts. Whenever you're in a crisis, stop, take a time-out, and get the facts. Never believe what you've heard. Find out if this is a real problem and if it is as grim as they say. Find out, because nothing is ever as bad as it seems initially; nothing is ever as good as it seems initially. Get the facts and ask questions. In fact, it's impossible to ask intelligent questions and be angry or upset at the same time. The very act of asking questions calms you down, activates your frontal lobe, and makes you see things clearly. It also calms everybody else down.

When real leaders face a big setback or difficulty, they say, "All right, let's sit down. What exactly has happened here, and how do we know that's true? Has anybody checked or corroborated that that is actually what happened? When did this occur?

How did this happen at this time? What are the exact steps that occurred, and who was involved in this? Whom could we talk to about resolving this? What steps can we take now? What could we do to minimize the damage?"

As you keep asking these questions, everybody settles down, and their frontal lobes activate as well. Pretty soon, you have a whole group of people thinking calmly, clearly, and rationally about immediate actions to minimize the cost of the crisis.

Another thing in crisis management is always to accept responsibility. When things go wrong, the natural tendency is to blame other people or circumstances, but if you do, you immediately become angry. All negative emotions are based on blame, and the antidote to blame is accepting responsibility.

People on my staff will come into my office and say, "I have this problem; this happened. These people cheated us."

I'll say, "Hold on. Calm down. You are responsible. This is your area of responsibility, so let's analyze this. What exactly happened? How did it happen? What are you going to do? What is your next step?"

Instead of having them hand the problem off to me, I turn it around and push it back into their hands.

Over time, they come back and calmly say, "There's this problem" (there are always problems in business). "This is what happened, and I am responsible, so this is what I've decided to do." Then they explain their plan of action and ask, "What do you think of that?"

I usually say, "That's very good." In most cases, they're closest to the problem, so their idea is better than anyone else's.

But sometimes I'll say, "I've seen this problem before, and you might think of doing this as well."

Suggestions on what to do when a crisis hits

- Take a deep breath and stay calm.
- Stop, take a time out, and get the facts.
- Always accept responsibility.

"Ah, that's a great idea. I hadn't thought of that."

They do that one additional thing, and they walk away proud, confident; their minds are clear and calm. There's no blame or anger from me.

Stuff happens in business. People cheat you, deals don't go through, sales don't work. Just stay calm and manage it. You can do this with any major problem in life. You can make the decision in advance that no matter what happens, you're going to remain calm and clear and ask questions. You're going to find a solution and act on it.

Divorces and Breakups

So far I've made these suggestions in the light of business crises, but they can work in personal crises as well.

Let's talk about divorce, or the breakup of a relationship. This can be an extremely traumatic event. In some cases, the couple can agree to go their own ways on friendly terms, but in other cases, it can be nasty. The lawyers get involved, and they want you to fight as long as possible so they can earn as many fees as possible. Lawyers earn their money from hourly fees. When you go to them with a problem, their goal is to run the meter up as much as possible before solving it. They'll want to do all kinds of depositions, research, and follow-up.

A divorce lawyer's job is to get you so spitting angry at the other person that you will run up the meter for a long time. They will get you to the point where you exaggerate everything bad that happened, how unjustified it was, and how you are entitled to massive damages and compensation. Be aware of that.

Here's the most important point. When two people enter into a relationship, they enter into it with the best of intentions. Many relationships don't work out because people change and evolve in the course of the relationship.

Most divorces take place when people are in their late twenties. They've gotten married in their early twenties, but in that decade, they go through the most rapid and dramatic changes in their lives. At the end of the decade, they're not the same people that entered into the marriage at the beginning. Consequently, they can find that they are no longer compatible with the other person.

The true test of compatibility is how much you laugh together. The first thing that goes in a relationship is laughter. The sex, actually, is the thing that goes last. You can be going to divorce court while you're still sleeping together, but the first thing that goes is the humor. You stop enjoying each other's company. When you're together, there are long periods of silence. You watch television. Sometimes you see couples go out for dinner. They sit there, and they don't talk to each other. They look off. They check their phones. They sit there and eat, and then they get up and leave.

Incompatibility is something that just happens. It rains, the sun comes up, the grasses grow, and incompatibility occurs between people. No one is to blame. No one is at fault.

The true test of compatibility in relationships is how much you laugh together.

Both people enter into the relationship with the best of intentions. But because human beings change, they become different people; they find that they are no longer compatible. If that's the case, you take a deep breath, and you say, "Look, this isn't working out. I don't dislike you; you don't dislike me. You are not to blame. You're not at fault. Nobody's wrong here." It's blaming that leads to all the turmoil in a divorce settlement.

As soon as you realize that you both gave it the best shot, but you're not cut out for each other, it means that you're probably better cut out for someone else. The sooner you end this marriage and get on with the rest of your lives, the sooner you'll find a place where you'll be happy.

Once you go through a divorce, there's going to be about a six-month period of healing. On average, it takes six months to heal after an emotional relationship has been terminated. So expect that.

Sometimes there is talk about rebound relationships. People have rebound relationships right after the marriage or relationship has ended. This rebound relationship is usually turbulent, unstable, and so on, but it's often how people readjust to reality. At the end of six months, they're back to being their normal selves, and life goes on.

With divorce, nobody is at fault. Nobody's to blame. You became incompatible, just as it rains. It's natural. No one is to be punished for it. Go your separate ways. Minimize the difficulties. Go to a lawyer who specializes in helping couples to come to a happy resolution in splitting up the property and possessions. Do it in a gentlemanly, or if you like, in an adult way.

Never do or say anything in a divorce settlement that you don't want to live with for years. Don't say negative things to other people. Never say them to your children or your friends. Always say, "He or she is an excellent person, but we found we were not suited for each other." That's the only thing you ever say, even if in your heart you're angry and disappointed.

Bankruptcy

Another issue is bankruptcy. Bankruptcy is very common. Most of the most successful people have been bankrupt. In fact, almost all wealthy people have been bankrupt, or almost bankrupt, two or three times. Henry Ford was bankrupt twice before he developed his motor car. By the time he was sixty, he had become the richest man in the world.

A bankruptcy is painful. First of all, you have to go through it. Go through it the best way you can, and remember that life is very long. Recognize that your reputation is the most important thing you have. Your reputation for dealing with money is very important, so if you go through a bankruptcy, treat everybody the best way you possibly can.

Do not sue. Do not accuse. Do not be angry. Just take it like an adult. It's s like taking a spanking. It's unfortunate. You did everything you possibly could. Maybe you started a business when you didn't have enough experience. Maybe the market fell out from underneath you. Whatever happened, it's over; it's done. All that matters now is how you carry yourself.

The most important thing in a bankruptcy is to ask, "What did I learn from this?" I have a good friend who went through a business bankruptcy when he was in his mid-twenties. He spent two or three years building this business. He worked sixteen hours a day. He had two partners. And the business failed. He had to move back in with his mother. It took him six months of mourning, six months of sitting around, watching television, before he got back on his feet. But during that time, he did one of the smartest things I've ever heard of. He got a spiral notebook, and he wrote down the answers to these questions:

What did I learn from this business experience?
What did I learn about people?
What did I learn about customers?
What did I learn about partners?
What did I learn about marketing?
What did I learn about money?
What did I learn about banks?
What did I learn about suppliers?
What did I learn about credit?

He would write down every lesson he'd learned in each of those categories. He came up with ten or twenty lessons.

I did this later myself when I was going through a bad business situation: I sat down and wrote down all the lessons. Once you do that, you're ten times less likely to have those problems again, because writing the lessons down programs them into your subconscious mind. When you see another situation that's similar, your subconscious mind tells you, "We've been here before." You can save yourself a fortune.

After six months writing down all these lessons and realizing what he had done right and what he would do differently, my friend started another business. Within a few years, he was a multimillionaire. He said, "Identifying all my mistakes from my bankruptcy made me wealthy. The business would never have succeeded anyway in the long term, but because it failed, it made me rich."

Job Loss

Then there's the loss of a job. Losing a job is God's way of telling you you're in the wrong position in the first place. Being fired is God's way of telling you you shouldn't even have had that job. So when you lose a job, consider it to be a blessing.

Peter Drucker said that keeping a person at a job in which they're incompetent is the cruelest thing you can do. If a person has no future at a job, and you've already decided that, let them go quickly. Let them go free so they can find a job they're better suited for.

Many managers think they're being compassionate by keeping a person in a job in which they're obviously incompetent. No, you're just being cowardly. You're not being compassionate; you're being cruel and hurtful to this person. You're keeping them away from real life, because when they finally do go (which they inevitably will), they're going to have to start over anyway. You're killing

---

"Keeping a person at a job in which they're incompetent is the cruelest thing you can do."
—Peter Drucker, management consultant & author

---

these people. You're robbing them of the most important thing in the world—their lives—by keeping them off the field, sitting on the bench in a game that they're never going to win.

Let them go free. Let them go freely. Help them. Give them support. Give them severance pay. Give them back everything, but let them go free.

The kindest, gentlest, most loving thing you can do with an employee who's not working out is to set them free so they can find the right place for themselves. I've probably spoken to a million managers worldwide over the years. Eyes open up like sunrises when I tell them this. They realize, "Yes, the reason I've been keeping that person there is that I didn't want to hurt them or their family."

When you let someone like this go, it often happens that this person will go to another company, get another job, and turn out to be a superstar. You'll say, "I fired that jerk two years ago, and look, he's now vice president of a fast-growing company." Well, of course, but he wasn't right for *your* job.

Deaths in the Family

The fourth area of crisis is the loss of a spouse or a child.

The most important thing here is, don't blame yourself for anything. Don't say, "If only I'd done this," or "I should have spent more time with him or her." Don't beat yourself up when someone in your family dies, because when they die, it's over. It's finished.

As with a divorce, it generally takes six months for you to recover from the loss of a family member. Many people take several years. Many others never recover. They just walk around with a pall of gloom over their heads.

That's not for you. You accept that the death has happened. Pray if you want. Go for a walk. Take some time off. Relax. Read some spiritual material. Give yourself time to heal.

It's like breaking a limb: it takes time to heal. But the most beautiful words in the English language, the four words that are always true for all people at all times under all circumstances, are: "This too shall pass."

Just say that. *This too shall pass.* It's very painful. It's hurtful. It's disappointing. You have all those what-ifs. But *this too shall pass.*

**As with a divorce, it generally takes six months
to overcome the loss of a family member.**

Life-Threatening Illness

The last crisis is a life-threatening diagnosis like cancer or heart disease. In 2010, I went to visit my doctor because I had a sniffle and runny nose. It had been going on for several weeks, so I thought I needed an antibiotic to zap it out.

"Brian," said the doctor, "I do not think you have a runny nose or an infection. I think you have throat cancer."

I was shocked. After all, I'm a professional speaker. I found that everybody who receives a cancer diagnosis goes into a period of shock, because the only thing they can think of is death— withering away and dying in great pain.

I walked out of the office stunned. That week I was interviewing two potential clients on the phone for speaking engagements. I was so wired and upset, I was almost shouting into the phone. Both of them said, "We don't want this guy anywhere near our people." It was the first time this had ever happened to me. Afterwards, I could see that I was so discombobulated with this diagnosis that I had to settle down.

I followed my own advice. Number one: stay calm. Number two: get the facts. I began to do enormous amounts of research. Over time I read more than thirty books on cancer. I went onto the websites; I checked every single part of WebMD, all the doctor sites, and everything on my type of cancer. I got all the information possible. I found that I had level 1, type 1 cancer. I had a melanoma in my throat.

Level 4 means it's over; select the roses for your funeral. Level 3 is the last chance, so you have to make it. I had level 1–level 2.

My doctors sat down and explained the standard treatment. They said, "First, we'll do a biopsy to check to make sure that there is a genuine cancer and what it is. Second, we do chemotherapy, which will shrink the entire cancer area. Third, we will do surgery to take out any remaining cancerous parts that we can find. Fourth, you'll have radiation, which is a way of killing any invisible cancer cells that don't show up in MRIs.

"It's a six-month process. Parts of it are quite uncomfortable and painful. You'll lose your hair. Your throat will burn out. You'll lose your ability to swallow. You will lose your ability to taste anything, but if you follow this course of treatment, at the end of six months, you'll be back speaking again."

I followed their course of treatment. I kept reading everything I possibly could. I read about all the bogus treatments that are all over the Internet, none of which have ever been validated by research, and I just followed the standard treatment. Six months later, I was speaking to 800 people in Singapore and got a standing ovation.

If you have a life-threatening disease, trust your doctors. They are not in this business to make a lot of money. People in the cancer industry especially have committed their lives to saving people and extending their lifespans. With heart disease, it's the same thing. In every major category, the people have dedicated their lives to helping their patients heal and live longer. So trust your doctors. Do what they tell you. Relax. Stay calm. Stay informed. Get information.

Good doctors will say, "Don't accept what I say. Go to another specialist; get a second opinion." I did that. I got second opinions from one of the finest cancer centers in the United States. They came back and said, "What your doctor has recommended is exactly correct." So just relax and say, "Take me." Six months later, I was speaking.

Again, stay calm. Get the facts. Take whatever actions you possibly can. Make adjustments. As the Marine Corps says, adjust, adapt, respond. Take whatever action you possibly can, but mostly stay calm.

Crisis Anticipation

The most important thing is to expect to have setbacks and difficulties throughout your life. One subject that I teach is called *crisis anticipation*: you sit down and say, "What are the worst possible things that can happen to me in the different parts of my life?" Use the 3 percent rule, which says that if there is a 3 percent possibility of this happening, you should think about it and plan for it.

Think about your health: disability, blindness, heart attack, if I lost my voice, if I were unable to walk, unable to work. Ask, what would be the worst thing that could happen, and what would I do if that were to occur?

The 3-percent Rule: If there's a 3 percent possibility of this
happening, you should think about it and plan for it.

First of all, you organize your health habits. You do everything
possible that you can, but you also make provision with insurance,
savings, disability payments, and everything else, so if this happens,
it's not going to destroy your family. You plan in advance. The mark
of the superior person is advanced planning and crisis anticipation.

The same goes for your business. What's the worst thing that
could happen? Your business could go bankrupt. All right. What
would be the first step you could take now to make sure that you
are protected against that? Or if you had a major reversal? Build
up cash reserves. It's one thing they tell you in every business book.
Once your business starts to grow, put everything back into it, and
build up cash reserves.

Expect dramatic down months. Expect crises. Don't spend
every penny you have and end up with an empty bank account in
the face of a crisis.

If you're thinking about your family, what's the worst thing
that can happen? You buy insurance. You buy safety seats for your
young children, and you buy the best seats possible so that if the
car flipped, your child would be safe.

We had a friend whose wife was on the phone once and was
talking away for half an hour. Then she turned around and
started looking for her child. She'd left the door open to the backyard. They had a plastic sheet over the Jacuzzi there, and this little
child, two years old, walked out and stepped on the sheet. The
child was sucked under the water, and, unable to move, drowned
at the bottom of the Jacuzzi.

This death destroyed their lives. It ended up in a divorce, and years later, they're still angry with each other and angry with themselves.

My children were never alone in their lives until they were old enough to drive. We put in higher locks so that they could never get out to the pool. We have grandchildren now, and we have safety locks, kid locks on everything. The kids cannot get into or touch anything where there may be any danger at all.

Why? It only has to go wrong once for a total trauma. Therefore, what are the worst things that could happen with your kids? Guard against them. Don't ever trust to luck. Hope is not a strategy. Wishing is not a strategy. Trusting to luck is not a strategy; it's a formula for disaster. Always guard against the worst things that could happen. Think them through and take the steps in advance.

If you're a speaker, never take the last flight for a speech the next day, because what if that flight is canceled? You can lose the whole talk. All the organizer's time is wasted. You're sitting on one side of the country, and you can't get there. So always take one or two flights before the last flight. Always get in early rather than late. Never cut it too close. Always buy time.

The smartest people play down the chessboard. Ask, "What are the worst things that can possibly happen, and if they did, how could I guard against them or minimize the cost?"

Ask yourself: What are the worst things that could possibly happen, and if they did, how could I ever guard against them or minimize the cost?

NINE

Motivating Others

If motivation is an inside job, it might sound like a contradiction in terms to talk about motivating others, but there's no doubt that some leaders do a better job of getting subordinates to perform better than others.

The most important human desire is to be happy, to have high self-esteem, to feel confident, to feel secure, to feel good about yourself and what you're doing. I've already talked about feeling like a winner. Excellent leaders make people feel like winners. The way to make people feel like winners is to set up a structure that enables them to win.

In a marathon, which is 26.2 miles, they have a mile meter at every mile so that when you are running, you can see it. You can hit the next meter, then the next. People win one mile at a time. If they only had one finish line, and you ran three hours for twenty-six miles without knowing how close or how far away you were, you would lose heart.

Florence Chadwick was the first woman to swim the English Channel. The first time she tried, she swam from France to

England, to the White Cliffs of Dover—the narrowest part. She swam and swam, and the fog came down and covered the water. About a mile away from her goal, she gave up. She had a support boat pull her in. She said later, "I could have made it if I could have just seen the other side. I didn't realize how close I was, but I didn't see the other side."

The next time Florence Chadwick swam the channel, they made sure that the weather would be clear all day long. She swam the channel, and became the most famous swimmer in history.

People need to swim a channel. They need to win. They need to succeed. One study, which may be the most profound study in managerial success ever done, looked at 22,000 businesses in twenty countries over ten years. These businesses were analyzed in terms of many different qualities and characteristics to find out what separated the most profitable companies from the least profitable.

Habits of Highly Successful Companies

To begin with, the researchers found that the most successful companies had clear goals and objectives at every level. Everybody knew exactly what their goal was, what they were expected to accomplish, and the results they were expected to get. They spent a lot of time talking about their goals and clarifying them. In other words, they knew where the finish line was.

The second characteristic of the most successful companies was that they had very clear measures, standards, and benchmarks. Every single job, and every part of every job, was measured, so that an employee always knew how close or how far away they were from achieving their goal—like a marathon runner.

The third factor was schedules and deadlines. Each person knew exactly what they needed to achieve, how it would be measured, and when it was expected to be accomplished.

In other words, the best companies set up everyone to be a winner. Every single person knew what they had to do to win. They knew exactly what it was, and they did it.

The fourth factor was very high rewards for excellent performance. This is called a *performance culture*. If a person not only meets, but exceeds, the expected quotas and standards, they get a bonus. If they do a good job, they get a great bonus.

Jack Welch became president of General Electric and managed it for twenty years. He took it from $5 billion in sales to $160 billion—one of the most profitable and successful companies in history. Soon after he began, he installed a performance culture. A top executive earning $500,000 a year to run a major division could earn $500,000 or a $1 million bonus at the end of the year by exceeding the expected accomplishments. So everybody in that company, including and especially the best people, drove themselves to exceed the numbers.

GE had four levels of accomplishment. The first was *average*: you completed your job, and everyone was happy. The second level was *excellent*: you had done your job at an excellent level, and it was recognized, and for that, you got a bonus—maybe 10 or 20 percent of your salary. The third level was *wow*. At *wow*, you got double your salary. Then they had *double wow*, and at *double wow* you got triple your salary.

Everybody in that company thought in terms of *wow* and *double wow*. Everybody wanted to win and win big. This company was in the paper almost every day as one of the fastest growing, most innovative, most profitable movers and shakers in the industry, and it was because all of these people had this mentality.

A good leader structures work so that people can win all the time. Every job, even small jobs, are very clear, with measurable results and deadlines.

In the Olympics, the greatest world records are set in front of the biggest audiences. In other words, you can't just run and come across the finish line: you've got to have the cheering of the crowds.

Similarly, the manager becomes the cheerleader. He praises, encourages, and rewards and makes it a big thing when people hit their targets, even little ones. The manager takes the person out for lunch, mentions this achievement at the staff meeting, and leads a hand of applause. "So-and-so did this last week, and boy, it was really hard. We know how tough it is out there. Let's give him or her a round of applause."

Everybody loves to applaud their fellow workers, and while they are, they're thinking, "I want to be the person who gets applause next time." The person who gets the applause can hardly wait to call home and tell their spouse, "Hey, you won't believe what happened to me today." For months, they remember the applause, praise, and encouragement that they got.

You may think, "This is pretty simple stuff." Yes, it is, and the best companies and the best leaders do it. This is the starting point of servant leadership: to make people feel important. Make them feel valuable. Make them feel worthwhile. Make them feel they are making a vital contribution to the company. This comes from you. It comes from the way you treat people.

Today 65–67 percent of employees do not feel fully engaged with their companies. They are looking out of the corner of their eye for a better job should it come along.

The 4 Habits of Highly Successful Companies

1. Clear goals and objectives at every level.
2. Very clear measures, standards and benchmarks.
3. Schedules and deadlines.
4. Very high rewards for excellent performance.

Overall, highly successful companies set up their employees to be winners.

Here are the things that you do to create an environment where people are fully engaged, love to come to work, and hate to leave the office. When they do leave, they leave with their coworkers, go with them to the bar or the restaurant, and talk about the work and the business." They are totally engaged. Those businesses are two or three times as productive, dollar for dollar, as the companies where people just go to work, do their jobs, leave at five, and don't think about it afterwards.

The Five Top Secrets

Some years ago, I was invited to speak for one of the biggest companies in the world. They said, "Before you speak to our managers, you should know what they have been trained in. Here is the workbook." It was numbered and categorized as Top Secret. "We will allow you to read this over the weekend," they said, "but you are not allowed to take notes, photocopy it, or duplicate it in any way. And you need to give it back on Monday."

So I sat down with this management program. It was about 300 pages, and I spent the whole weekend with it. This company had fanned out worldwide and studied 120 teams in their worldwide operation that had accomplished extraordinary things. They had reduced the costs of a highly competitive product by 80 percent; speeded the time to market to six months rather than one year; dramatically increased sales and profitability by 300–500 percent.

The company hired consultants to determine the common denominators of these winning teams and put them together into this extensive program. They taught this formula for success to every up-and-coming executive in the company.

I was so impressed that I said, "I would love to be able to teach this to my business audiences."

They said, "No, this is top secret. We spent a fortune figuring these things out."

"What could I do to go around this?"

"You could write a letter to the president."

I wrote a letter to the president of this company, and I got a reply back giving me permission to teach these ideas—not the whole process, but the ideas that were essential for business leaders. I'm the only person in the world that has ever been given the permission to teach them.

Here are the five principles in this incredible process.

SHARED VALUES

Principle number one was *shared values*. Everybody sits down and talks about the culture. Your culture is based on the values that you have in common. Sit down and ask, "What are our values? What do we believe in and stand for? What will we not compromise?"

The values, as we saw earlier, can be fairly simple: honesty and integrity, quality products and services, excellent customer service, respect for others, profitability, and so on.

In the best companies, they would all sit down and come up with a consensus about the three to five core values of their business. They said, "We may change products and services and markets and sales and profits, but we never deviate from these values. Is that agreed?" Everybody agreed. So that's number one. That's the heart of the culture of a business.

There is a program in America called the Malcolm Baldrige National Quality Award. This was founded by Malcolm Baldrige when he was the secretary of commerce under Ronald Reagan. He noticed that there was a special Deming Prize in Japan, which was awarded for the highest-quality companies.

W. Edwards Deming was an American who preached the idea of quality control. He was ignored in this country in the fifties and sixties, so he went to Japan and preached his idea there. It transformed the Japanese economy, making it the number three economy in the world. The highest award that you can get in Japan for a company is a Deming Prize.

Baldrige said we should have something like that in America. So the government established the Baldrige Award. The Baldrige Award has a thirty-, forty-page questionnaire that you have to fill out. You have to add $350,000 to cover the costs of all the investigation that they will do. Then they will come, and they'll fan out into your company. They'll talk to your customers, your suppliers, your staff at all levels; they'll talk to your executives; they'll talk to the people in the financial markets to see if this really is a high-quality company.

One question the investigators ask is, what are the core values of this business? Here's the rule: they have to be able to ask any-

---

Every employee at every level of your company should be able to answer the question: *What are the core values of this company?*

---

body at any level of the company, and the person must be able to respond immediately. They could be interviewing a janitor on the loading dock and ask, "What are the core values of this company?" The janitor should be able to stand up and say, "Our core values are truth, integrity, quality service, and respect for the individual." If they ask anyone in the company and that person does not know the values, they tear up your application and keep the $350,000, because you are obviously not a quality company. That was the starting point.

SHARED GOALS AND OBJECTIVES

Number two is *shared goals and objectives*. People in the company would sit down, talk about, plan, and agree on their goals—how they would be measured, when they were due, and what would be required of everyone to achieve them.

SHARED PLANS OF ACTION

Number three was *shared plans of action*. They would all agree on who was going to do what and when and to what standard, and they were all committed to fulfilling their responsibility. Everybody agreed that they would all fulfill their responsibilities and that everybody would know what everyone else was doing.

CONTINUOUS REVIEW OF PERFORMANCE

Step number four was *continuous review of performance*, both internal and external. They would sit down with each other and ask,

"How are we doing? How is everything going?" The discussions were always open. People would say, "You didn't do this, and you said you would have this done."

Everything was done openly and above board. There was no politics, no cliques. If somebody said they were going to do it, they would do it.

LEADING BY EXAMPLE

Number five was *leading by example.* The head of the team was what they call the orchestra conductor type of leader. Not like the coach, who shouts at people to run the ball. Not like the military officer, who gives people orders. Not like the professor, who operates on a consensual basis with his peers. The leaders would lead the action and saw themselves as the facilitators. Their job was to make it possible for everyone else to do their job. They would ask them, "What do you need to do your job? Do you need extra equipment or people or resources? Do you need time? Do you need funds to be able to travel?" The manager saw himself as the leader who made it possible for everyone else to do their work.

Summary of the 5 Top Secrets of Winning Teams

1. Shared values.
2. Shared goals and objectives.
3. Shared plans of action.
4. Continuous review of performance.
5. Leading by example.

The Big Three

I have trained companies all over the world with these five principles, and it's astonishing. They come back and say, "We've revolutionized our business. We thought everybody knew the values, but when we sat down, nobody was clear. We thought that everybody knew our goals and objectives, but when we asked people to be specific, nobody could say. They all had their own different versions."

Here's an example that I give in my seminars. I say there is a law of three in the world of work. This law says that there are three things that you do that contribute 90 percent of your value in your work; everything else you do is in the other 10 percent. Therefore one of the great keys to success is to do the Big Three.

The way to determine the Big Three is to ask, if you could only do one thing for your business all day long, which would be the most important thing that you could do? What would make the greatest contribution? I have people think about that and write it down.

Then I say, "All right, now imagine you could only do two things all day long. What would be the second biggest contributor of value to your business and to yourself?"

That takes a little bit more time. Finally, I say, "If you could only do three things all day long, what would be number three?"

This exercise takes about ten to fifteen minutes until people are clear. Then I say, "The next thing you need to do is check with your boss and your coworkers and make sure that your idea is consistent with theirs."

Many managers will go back and say, "These are my Big Three," and the people around them will say, "No, they're not.

The *Big Three*: If you could only do three things all day long, what are the tasks that would make the greatest contribution of value?

That's not your job at all. *This* is your job." Your boss will say, for example, "The most important thing you should be doing is meeting with our key clients on a regular basis, face-to-face, but it's not even on your list."

I had a top executive come through one of my courses. I taught about goals and the Law of Three. It's a full-day program, but at 2:00 he got up, took his briefcase, and walked out. I went out, caught him, and said, "Tom, where are you going?"

He said, "I'm done."

"I unconditionally guarantee this program."

"No, I'm not going to exercise the guarantee. I've got my money's worth. Two life concepts: writing down my goals, picking my most important goal, and working on it every day, and practicing the Law of Three. I'll double my income by the end of the month just on those two. I don't need to hear any more." And he did. He tripled and quadrupled his income, and in the years ahead, he became a millionaire and retired early, just by setting clear goals, having one big goal, and focusing on the Big Three.

There are three rules with your Big Three tasks:

1. Do fewer things; stop doing things. You cannot get your life under control except to extent that you stop doing small things. I've already discussed A tasks versus the tasks. Stop doing the B task.

2. Do the Big Three more of the time. Do those takes all day long, and don't do anything else until you've exhausted all possibilities, which probably will never happen.

3. Get better at your three most important tasks. It's the greatest of all time savers. I worked with people in many different fields. I've helped them to identify the three most important things they do, and then to develop a learning program for each of those three. They've increased their income ten and twenty times over the next couple of years by focusing on excelling at the most important things they do, because the only thing that stands between you and extraordinary accomplishment is additional skills.

Keep Your Job

Then I'll say to the managers, "Now I would like to invite you to play a game with me, and the game is called Keep Your Job. Before you agree to play with me, let me tell you the rules. I'm going to ask you to write down the names of the people who report to you— your subordinates, your staff, your team—and I'm going to ask you to write down next to those names the three most important things they can do to make the most valuable contribution in their work. You'll write this all down. Then I'm going to take your list, and I'm going to ask your employees the three most important things they do in their work. If their answers and your answers are the same, you get to keep your job. Does anybody here want to play?"

I've done this for tens of thousands of managers. I've never had anyone in the world raise their hand. Nobody wants to play if those are the rules of the game. But the cruelest thing that you can do as a manager is leave people hanging and not knowing the three most important things they could be doing, and in order. The most generous, the most loving, the most positive thing you can do is take the time, all the time, to make sure everybody knows the most important thing that they can do.

I tell managers to do this: "When you get back, have a why-am-I-on-the-payroll? meeting. Have everybody write down the three most important things—their *primary* activities and responsibilities. Then below, you have them write down their three *secondary* responsibilities—the things they do after they've done the Big Three. Then everybody comes to a meeting with photocopies for everyone else. Then you go around, and everybody else discusses everybody's job."

So one employee says, "This is what I think my primary three are, and this is what I think are my secondary three." And everyone looks at these lists, and they discuss her job, and they say, "Yes," or "No, that's not your job; that's *my* job." They find there's overlap: two people think the same thing is their job. There's underlap, where nobody thinks it's their job. There's confusion, where people think they're supposed to be doing two totally different jobs. There's contradiction, where if you do one job, you can't do the other job.

You get this all worked out. Everybody comes out of the meeting absolutely clear about their Big Three and their secondary jobs, and they go back to work. The whole business transforms. It's like electricity.

Then we say, "All right, how do we measure it, and when is it due?" And we go around and we agree, or sometimes everybody's confused. One person says, "I had no idea that I had to have this done in a week. I didn't know that this had a deadline on it." Other people say, "Of course it's got a deadline. If you don't do that, everything stops in this other area."

Everybody develops our favorite word: *clarity, clarity, clarity.* Once everybody's clear, they are happy and motivated, because you've told them this is how you win, and you can win every day. It dramatically reduces the amount of chitchat and wasted time and checking email, because you don't get any joy from checking your email, but you do get joy from task completion.

The boss's job is to make sure that everybody has the resources they need to do their jobs, and then to cheer and applaud—to be the company cheerleader, walking around, telling people how good they are; congratulating people; telling them what a great job they did and how much they're appreciated. This raises the standards, but it also raises morale. It makes people excited about coming to work, because they can start and finish tasks. Their self-esteem and self-confidence go up. Their brains release endorphins, they feel happy and creative and are more personable and positive.

We have thirty people working in my company. You walk in, and you'll see that everybody is happy. They laugh and joke all the time. They're smiling. They're busy. They're good friends with one another. They're not wasting time chatting, but they do have meetings at which they talk to each other and share ideas. The spirit in that office is unbelievable, and they are generating more sales and profits than they ever dreamed possible.

Servant Leadership

There's a type of leadership that's been popularized in recent times under the name *servant leadership.*

The leader I've been discussing fits this role in many respects. The purpose is to serve the employees' highest needs, release their

---

The three words that lead to happy and motivated employees is *clarity, clarity, clarity.*

---

hidden energy and potential, and help the people in the organization to grow.

This is not to be mistaken for weakness. Some people try to operate on the basis of democracy and consensus: "Let's all get along, and let's all be friends." They are more concerned with being liked by their coworkers or employees than they are in the results.

Studies have shown that the best management style is that of the *benevolent dictator.* This expression came out of years of work by William Redding. It refers to a leader who is clear about the results he wants everybody to achieve, but who is still a nice person. He treats people with respect; he always says please and thank you; he's very clear that this job has to be done. "This is your job. It has to be done by this time. I will give you all the help and resources possible, but this is your job, and it must be done."

Someone may say, "I've got my kid's soccer game, and I was planning to go shopping." The benevolent dictator says, "That's fine. You can do that after work, but this job has to be done by this time and to this standard of quality. Are we clear about that? If there's a problem with that, we understand. You can go somewhere else if there's a problem with getting the job done on time."

Every breach of discipline leads to other breaches of discipline. Every weakness in dealing with employees demoralizes everyone else. If I'm working hard to do a good job, but I notice that somebody else can go off to soccer games or shopping, I'll say, "Why am I working my butt off? Why don't I just lean back?"

The person you're letting off the hook also becomes weaker, because they know that you will never be firm with them. The others, who are hard workers, become less and less motivated, because they know it doesn't make any difference: you can work yourself silly, and you still get the same rewards as people who are coasting.

In the best companies, everybody knows who the leader is, and the leader is very clear about what needs to be done and the way it needs to be done. They're friendly and supportive, and they give congratulations, thanks, and help, but they do not relent on the need to get the job done and get it done properly.

It's only then that people can feel like winners. Sometimes people need to be forced to complete their tasks, or they need to be urged or coerced, but it's only then that they can make their full contribution to the company. Then they feel wonderful about themselves, they feel happy, and they laugh.

Another study asked tens of thousands of employees, "Who is the best boss you ever worked for?" The second question they asked was, "Which qualities in this person made him or her the best boss you ever worked for?"

Two qualities emerged: the two C's. The first was *clarity*. "I always knew what my boss expected me to do. It was never ambiguous. He always made it clear what needed to be done, and when and in what order." Number two was *consideration*. "My boss always treated me like I was a person, aside from being an employee. My boss always asked me questions about myself and was concerned about my well-being and my family."

So those two: clarity and consideration. Being crystal clear about what needs to be done, and then being a friendly, helpful, and supportive person, and caring about your staff.

The Two C's of Great Bosses: *Clarity* and *Consideration.*

One example was Intel's Andrew Grove. People said he was one of the toughest people to work for in the computer industry. He cut no corners. He told you straight what he thought. Yet people enjoyed working for him, because he brought out the best in them. There was no nonsense. He would chop you to pieces if you had not done your homework or completed your tasks, but people said they grew more and became more competent. They were happier working for Andrew Grove than in any other job they ever had, although they said, "Boy, but he was a bastard to work with."

He set things up so that the workers were always winning, and he insisted that they win. He drove them to get results beyond anything they'd ever done, so they won. Then he would be full of praise; he'd give them bonuses and everything else.

One of the great leaders today, surprisingly, is Mark Zuckerberg of Meta (formerly Facebook). Mark has a 5:1 question to answer ratio. He's always asking questions. He doesn't talk, he doesn't preach, he doesn't say, "Do this," or lecture, but he's always asking questions, and you'd better have the answers. He will ask another question, and a follow-up question, and another follow-up question. He will help people become clearer and clearer about who they are, what their job is, and what they are expected to do.

Google is consistently considered to be one of the best companies in the world to work for. Not because you sit around and do nothing, but because everybody is focused on getting results. When you get results, you feel great. Your coworkers respect you, and you get promoted and you get paid more. When you say, "I work at Google," it's one of the highest accreditations you can have, because Google sets such high standards. If he works at Google—or at Apple, or any one of these companies—he must be really good.

Good bosses have high standards. They insist that people complete their tasks on time. They give them rewards; they give them praise; they give them approbation; they give them time off and ping-pong games and free food, but it's all tied to getting the job done so you can feel like a winner.

People are committed to the work to the degree to which they have a chance to discuss it. If you announce the job and say, "Please do this," their commitment is very low. It's not even *their* job, it's *your* job. They're helping you out. If you say, "This job needs to be done; how do you think we should approach it? How do you suggest that we handle it?" You involve them in a discussion. When they walk away, you have transferred ownership of the job from you to them. They will then take total responsibility so as not to disappoint you.

Here are the two most important qualities of great companies, according to the website A Great Place to Work: Number one is *trust*. There's a very high level of trust in the workplace. Everybody trusts each other, so they're spontaneous, and happy, and they share ideas. Number two is, *everybody feels in the know*. They feel that they're always kept up-to-date. They know everything that's going on in the business. There are no secrets, no closed doors. There are no cliques. Nothing is confidential. Everything is wide open. These are the two most important things that a manager can bring to a workplace for workers at any level. And that's particularly true for millennials and Generation X.

The Self-Made Leader

Perhaps the most important thing I ever learned about leadership was from Drucker, who was asked, are leaders born or are they made? He said, "There may be born leaders, but they are so few that they make no difference in the great scheme of things. Leaders are made. Leaders are self-made. They are self-made by work on themselves, and every person can develop themselves into a leader. A leader is a person who accepts responsibility for results. If you accept responsibility for results, you can become a leader with no followers. But if you accept responsibility for results, and you get the results that people are depending upon, you will soon have other people working with you to help you to get more and more results. You job is to become a multiplication sign so that you get great results. Then, when you are given assistants to work with you, working with them, you get more and more results."

TEN

The Power of Rituals

When I began to study time management, some people would say to me, "If you manage your time too tightly, you become too rigid. You're not flexible, you're not spontaneous, you're not enjoyable."

I investigated that idea very carefully, and I found that it's exactly the opposite. The more things in your life that you can make automatic, so that you don't even think about doing them, the more you can free your mind for higher-level activities. The more things that are automated, the more you can use your mind to achieve more of your goals, so when you get up in the morning you don't ask, "How do I put toothpaste on my toothbrush? How do I make the eggs?" You do them unthinkingly, and it frees up your mind for more important things.

The more things in your life that you can make automatic, so that you don't even think about doing them, the more you can free your mind for higher-level activities.

Successful people develop rituals that enable them to perform at a far higher level. I've given you my ritual for increasing your income 1,000 percent—2 percent a month, 25 percent a year, ten times in ten years.

I've had thousands of people come back to me and say, "Once you get into the rhythm of getting up early, rewriting your goals, studying and upgrading your skills, planning your day in advance, and so on, you get so much more done with so little stress that you look forward to doing it. It becomes automatic and easy."

It's very hard to develop a habit initially, but then it's very easy to live with. It's very difficult to discipline yourself over and over again, but then it locks in and it becomes automatic. You just do it without thinking about it.

Get Enough Sleep

Successful people have success rituals. First of all, going to bed and getting up. As I've said, your ability to thoroughly rest your mind, your brain, and your body has an incredible effect on your whole day. Remember, you are a thinking machine. All day long you solve problems and make decisions. One great idea is enough to make you rich. One great decision can transform a business. One problem solved can enable you to make more progress in a couple of years than many people make in many years.

So, first of all, go to bed early; get up early. You've heard it from Benjamin Franklin: "Early to bed and early to rise makes a man healthy, wealthy, and wise." Often we don't go to bed early because we get distracted by television, so the rule is, turn off the television by 9:00 so that your brain can unwind, and go to bed at 10:00.

> "Early to bed and early to rise makes a man healthy, wealthy, and wise." —Benjamin Franklin, Founding Father

A recent study has found that rich people watch less than one hour of television a day, and they usually watch it prerecorded on their own schedule. If you watch television before you go to bed, it can scramble your mind.

Another thing: you should eat three hours before bedtime, because that enables the food to digest, and it enables you to fall asleep. If you eat any closer to sleep time, it can keep you awake and give you bad sleep, so you're in bed for the same number of hours but you wake up tired out, dragging yourself. Be very alert and jealous about getting enough sleep: think about it, plan it, organize it, put other things aside.

I have some good friends, who are very successful. When we were younger, we would go out for dinner at 8:00 or 9:00, eat and drink until 10:00 or 11:00, and go home at midnight. He and his wife now eat dinner at 5:00 or 6:00, and they go to bed at 8:00, or 9:00 at the very latest. They get up at 4:00 or 5:00, and they work, and they have a tremendously productive working day. If you get eight, nine, even ten hours of sleep at night, you are much more productive the following day. So make it a ritual to go to bed early and get up early.

I always advocate making a list of everything you have to do the night before. Go over your list, organize it, and have it in your mind. One of the main reasons we don't go to sleep is that we stay awake tossing and turning, thinking about something that we have to do tomorrow that we forgot to write down. When you write down everything, it clears your mind completely, like wiping a whiteboard, because everything you have to do tomorrow is written down.

Writing things down also taps into the powers of your mind. Your subconscious mind and your superconscious will work on that list all night. Often when you wake up in the morning, you'll have a perfect insight about how to solve a problem or achieve a goal. When you write down your goals for the day the night before, all night your incredible subconscious computer is working to bring you ideas. Many of the greatest breakthroughs in life, including scientific breakthroughs, happen to people who have woken up, sometimes in the middle of the night, with an idea that's changed their lives.

Always have a pad of paper and a pencil or pen on your nightstand, so, if you wake up in the night with a great idea, you can write it down, because if you don't, it will disappear. There's a rule from Napoleon Hill: "Catch the idea and write it down." Imagine the idea is flying through the air like a comet. Catch the idea and write it down. Sometimes that idea will change your life.

Exercise When You Get Up

A second ritual, which I practice every day, is to exercise when you get up in the morning. Professional physiotherapists say that if you are a morning exerciser, you're more likely to stay with your program and get all of its benefits. If you exercise later in the day, you're much more likely to make excuses. You're tired. You're busy. It's late. I get up in the morning and immediately exercise for fifteen to fifty minutes. At the very least, I will do a whole series of stretching exercises, sit-ups, and core exercises.

Everyone should do between 100 and 200 sit-ups every morning. This is one muscle you can't wear out. The way you do these—I learned this from an athletic specialist—is to put your hands behind your head, you pull your knees up with your feet flat on the floor, and just raise your shoulders. You don't go any further than that. You don't have to do Marine sit-ups, where you're crunching. All you have to do is get your shoulders off the floor, which tightens up your muscles. Almost anyone can do that ten, twenty, fifty, or 100 times. When you exercise your core, you strengthen your whole body and your posture, you feel better, and you have fewer pains in your back, hips, knees, and shoulders.

My favorite exercise is called the wig-wag. You lie on the floor on your back and you pull your knees up, and your feet are flat on the floor. Then you turn your knees as far as possible to one side and your head to the other, and then to the one side, and your head to the other. I do that thirty times, I do 150 to 200 sit-ups, and then I do the wig-wag thirty times more.

This completely exercises your full spine from your neck to your coccyx. Your whole spine is being rotated sixty times every day. It's completely noninvasive. It takes no muscular strength. But it's one of the greatest guarantors that you'll never have back problems. Today back problems are experienced by 50 percent of people past the age of forty. It's because they don't continually rotate their spines.

I also aerobic exercise, which is essential. If you do aerobic exercises in the morning, you are brighter, sharper, and more creative, and you have more energy all day long. I have my own treadmill, my own elliptical machine, and my own exercise bicycle. Plus I have a pool across the street at the country club, which has 72 feet per lap.

You need 200-300 minutes of exercise each week, and you plan it the same way you would a business meeting.

You need about 200–300 minutes of exercise each week, and you plan it the same way you would a business meeting. "This morning I get up, and I do this set of exercises," and then maybe you add on aerobic exercises. "I swim twice a week, half a mile a swim, one mile a week. I set the date, I set the time, and I get up in the morning, and I go and do it."

I joke with my wife that I wake up at 6:00 or 6:30, grab myself by the scruff of the neck and throw myself into the pool before I know what's happening. Then I thrash back and forth. This keeps you pumped all day long.

If you exercise on a regular basis, you start to inject endorphins, nature's happy drug, into blood and brain. If you take any drug repeatedly, eventually you develop an addiction. And the finest addiction you can develop is to endorphins, because you can only get endorphins when you do something that is life-enhancing. When you laugh, love, walk, read something that you enjoy, write down your goals, and especially when you do aerobic exercise, you activate endorphins, and you feel good for hours. If you do this repeatedly, soon you become addicted to getting up in the morning and exercising. Soon you have to resist the temptation to do it, because you start to look forward to how good you're going to feel afterwards.

Meditation

Another ritual for success is to meditate for fifteen minutes every day. Meditation is not easy for me, although spiritual reading, solitude, and contemplation is very enjoyable. (But here's the danger with meditation: 50–70 percent of meditators just fall back to sleep.)

Then you take something that is educational, motivational, or spiritual—a single chapter in a book will do—and you read it and think about how you could apply it to your day. As the great preacher Henry Drummond observed, "The first hour is the rudder of the day." Whatever you put into your mind in the first hour sets you up for the whole day. This is why you must avoid reading the news and all the garbage about rapes, murders, and corruption first thing in the morning, because that will set you up for negativity.

Read something that's positive and uplifting for the first fifteen minutes to thirty minutes each day, and then you can do something else. After exercising, I like to start the day with a cup of coffee. Combine a cup of coffee with reading something uplifting, underlining—never read without a pen in your hand so that you can underline—and it's almost like taking a spiritual pill. You feel happy. You feel ready for the day, and you're far more creative.

"The first hour is the rudder of the day."
—Henry Drummond, Preacher

Write Down Your Priorities

Write down six priorities each day. Buy a spiral notebook, open it up, and write today's date and place, along with ten goals, in the present tense, as I've already described. You can write down more than ten, but you must write down at least ten every day.

I used to offer a coaching program, and I would guarantee that if you came to me one day every three months and went through one solid day of exercises with me in planning, productivity, focus, and concentration, you would double your income *and* double your time off in one year. If you didn't, I would give you your money back. There would be no charge for the year. I never had a request for a refund.

In my coaching program, I always front-loaded the first day with ideas that are guaranteed to double people's incomes. First, I'd have everybody write down ten goals. Then I would hand out a spiral notebook and say, "This is going to be your new best friend. For the next thirty days, I'm going to ask you to do just this one thing: open this up every morning, and write down your ten goals without reference to what you wrote yesterday. You're not copying your ten goals. You're starting over again with a clean page by memory. And the most remarkable thing is going to happen. Some of the goals you wrote down during the first day will fall off the list. You'll forget to rewrite them, because they're not that important. Other goals will move down. Others will move up the list, and you will write them with even greater clarity. You'll rephrase the goals, develop new ones, and start to achieve them."

One of my students did this exercise with me on a Friday, and by Thursday of the next week he had accomplished five of his ten goals for the year. He said he could not believe it. It was like pushing down on a dynamite detonator. Everything exploded—business goals, life goals, family goals, friendship goals, money goals. It all just started to happen at an incredible rate. He said, "I achieved more in one week with those ten written goals than I expected to achieve in a year or two."

I would say to my students, "It takes three minutes to five minutes to write down your ten goals. Just do it for one month, and see what happens." I've had countless people say they've made

---

Write down your ten goals every morning for one month, and watch what happens.

---

more progress with this one idea than from three years of courses, coaching, and classes.

Try it out. Your whole life will begin to change. From then on, if it works, do this every morning as a ritual: get up, do your exercise, do your spiritual reading, write down your ten goals. That list of ten goals sets you up for the day. It activates your subconscious and superconscious. It activates your reticular cortex, which is the device in your brain that causes you to notice things that you hadn't noticed before. If you write down "I want to drive a brand-new Mercedes-Benz, black, silver, four-door, with leather upholstery," from that moment on you're going to see black Mercedes everywhere, and you're going to see different things that you can do to acquire the funds that you need to buy one.

Email Is Dessert

Another ritual has to do with email. Don't check your email in the morning: your email, as I said, is a dessert activity. Resist the temptation to get up in the morning and check your email. Some people have become so addicted to email that they get up in the night to check it. They even leave their cell phone on so it wakes them up throughout the night. They don't want to miss anything.

Why is this? It has to do with addiction. Whenever a bing goes off telling you you've got mail, it's like a slot machine. A little bit of dopamine shoots across your brain. Dopamine is the same stimulant that is in cocaine and other bad drugs. It stimulates you, alerts you, and makes you jump, so you immediately check your email.

That's why people leave their email and their phones on all day. Whenever they go off, it gives them a jolt, and they have to check. If they get low on jolts, they send out emails to their friends, who reply to them, and they get a jolt back. So if you check your email first thing in the morning, you get addicted to dopamine.

With alcoholism, they say, "One drink is too many, and none is enough." If you're an alcoholic, you cannot drink one drink. That's why they have Alcoholics Anonymous meetings at drinking time—7:00 in the evening. You meet with your group, and you stay there for two hours or three hours chatting, until the habitual time for having a drink has passed. Then you go home, and maybe you'll be OK. But if you have one drink, you cannot stop drinking until you pass out.

It's the same thing with dopamine. Once you get your first shot, you cannot stop checking your email all day long. The average adult checks their email 145 times a day. The average college student checks their email and social media eighteen times an hour. They usually move while they're hooked up to their phone, so they've got earphones, so they can hear every bing. They have different rings for different people, so they know, "Oh, that's Susan calling me." They're being jolted all the time, and they can't concentrate.

Dopamine is the anticoncentration drug. As I said before, all success comes from task completion: taking an important task and concentrating single-mindedly on it until it's complete. If you want to be rich and successful, start with your most important task every morning, and stay with it until it's complete before you do anything else. If you can discipline yourself to work flat out for two sessions of ninety minutes and complete one major task, your life will change. You'll engage in neuroplasticity. You'll reshape and reform the channels of your brain. You'll develop whole new ways of acting and thinking through repetition.

Over the last ten years, neuroscience has discovered that the brain is infinitely plastic, really until the eighth or ninth decade of life. If you feed yourself with new information, the brain develops new neural channels, and you begin to think, and respond, and act differently. You can transform your life by doing things repeatedly.

The best time manager say that many managers' careers are being ruined by an obsession with email. Now they have coaches and counselors that work with executives in Fortune 500 companies that sit there and say, "Stop it. Don't do it. Put it away." At first they're like drunks—they just keep reaching, almost spasmodically, for their iPhones, or checking their email. Turn it off, shut it down, leave it off. One great rule, from Thomas Moore, the philosopher and author of *Care of the Soul*, is, leave things off. Leave off the television. Leave off the computer. Leave off the iPhone. Leave things off, and create silence.

Tim Ferriss wrote a book called *The Four-Hour Work Week*. When he started off, he was working fourteen hours a day, seven days a week, checking emails. By the time he finished, he was checking his emails once a week, and he'd tripled his income. He

---

"Leave things off. Leave off the television.
Leave off the computer. Leave off the iPhone.
Leave things off, and create silence."
—The great rule of Thomas Moore, author

---

takes three or four months of vacation each year, he travels around the world, he's learned new subjects and new languages, and he's never made more money in his life.

Tim explains the process of setting up a virtual assistant or an executive assistant. He has a virtual assistant in the Philippines, and all his emails go to her. He has a list of frequently asked questions, so if people write and ask one of these, she just plugs in the answer. If it's an emergency, she sends it on to him, wherever he happens to be. He said that over time, there have been fewer and fewer emergencies that his virtual assistant can't handle.

The Most Important Meal

Eat a nutritious breakfast. There's a wonderful expression, "Well begun is half done." Your mother told you that breakfast is the most important meal of the day, because the food that you eat in the morning gives you the energy that you need to run your day. It's almost like starting off on a trip with an empty tank of gas. When you wake up in the morning, your tank is empty; your glucose levels are low. So you have to fill your tank, and what you fill your tank with largely determines the quality of your day.

Some years ago a man named Barry Sears wrote a book called *The Zone*. It became one of the best-selling books on diet in history, and it's life-transforming. He said that every food you take is a chemical. Every chemical has side effects. If you drink a Coke or a Red Bull, or eat toast or bacon, these have side effects. So eat the foods that are the most perfectly balanced to give you the highest level of energy for the longest period of time. These are proteins. So in the morning you eat eggs, but you don't eat toast or bagels.

One rule for success is eliminate the three white poisons: sugar, flour, and salt. The average American consumes something like twenty or thirty pounds of sugar each year. They take in sugar in candies and in Cokes. One can of Coke, by the way, has twelve tablespoons of sugar. A big Slurpee may have almost a cup of sugar in it. We have an obesity epidemic because people are drinking huge quantities of soft drinks. Of course, the sugar builds up, so you have a 36 percent obesity rate in America today. We are the fattest people in the world. In fact, an expression came out of Harvard: *Porcus Americanus*. When I go to Europe, I've started to talk about a proper diet, but there are no fat people in the audience, so I say, "I think I'll just pass over this one. It's not necessary for you to hear."

Start off with a high protein diet, such as eggs, and complex carbohydrates, which means fruits and vegetables. That will give you enough energy to run for five straight hours. At lunchtime, eat salads with protein. Don't eat salads with carbohydrates, no breads, no pastries, no cakes, no Cokes, no anything else—salad with protein. It can be salad with fish, steak, chicken, or tofu. That will give you five hours more of high energy without afternoon drowsiness.

People go into an afternoon slump. In the southern countries they have a siesta. They sleep for two hours, because they eat huge pasta, bean, and tortilla lunches. But if you have only protein and complex carbohydrates, fruits and vegetables, for breakfast and lunch, you will have high levels of energy, your glycemic index will be high, and your brain will be functioning at maximum all day long.

Eliminate the three white poisons: *Sugar, Flour and Salt.*

If you get into the habit of doing these things, you will produce twice as much as the person next to you who comes back from lunch drowsy after a heavy meal and whose brain is half-functioning. Many companies are developing sleeping rooms so when people come back from lunch after an hour, they can sleep, because they're useless anyway.

I've just discussed a low-carb diet. Barry Sears found that if you mix in a carbohydrate, like bread, pastry, pasta, rice, even potatoes, with a protein, the carbohydrate causes your body to release alkalines, and the protein causes your body to release acids. When you have a lunch that has proteins and carbohydrates, your body rushes alkalines and acids into your stomach to break them down.

An acid and an alkaline neutralize each other, so the digestive process stops. Your body goes into a form of emergency and says, we've got to get more blood in there, we've got to start rushing more blood to the stomach to break down this food. You start to burp and feel bloated, and the blood is rushed away from your muscles and your brain. You start to feel drowsy and dumb.

That's why they tell you never go swimming an hour after eating: the digestive process is pulling blood away from your muscles, so you'll have cramps and can even drown.

If you discipline yourself to eat more proteins and fresh fruits and vegetables, you'll have high energy all day long. So make that a habit.

Elite Performance

At work, focus on your strengths and delegate your weaknesses. The Law of Three says there are three things that you do that contribute 90 percent of your value in your work. One great key to success is to do the Big Three. Resolve to be in the top 10 percent in each of these three areas, and pay any price, go any distance, make any sacrifice to achieve it.

Dr. Anders Ericsson at the University of Florida has put twenty-five years of research into elite performance, and his work's been quoted by lots of people. He's the one who came up with the idea that it takes 7,000 hours to achieve elite performance. However, subsequent research proves that if you have a natural talent or ability in a particular field, you can achieve elite performance in the top 5 or 10 percent in a year or two. It doesn't take seven years if you already have a natural ability.

Researchers have looked at income and socioeconomic mobility, asking, why do some people earn so much more than others? They all started off at the same starting line at the beginning of their careers. They started running, like in a marathon, but over the years, some people got much further ahead in the income race. Eighty percent or more stayed in the middle, with average income, and a small percentage fell behind.

The researchers looked at the people who got far ahead. The 80/20 rule holds. Some people got into the top 20 percent, where they were earning more than people in the bottom 80 percent. But then there's the top 20 percent of the top 20 percent, which is the top 4 percent. These people were earning something like thirty-two times the average of the people in the bottom 80 percent. Then they took the top 20 percent of the top 20 percent of the top 20 percent, which is the top 0.4 percent, and these people were earning over fifty times the average of the people in the bottom 80 percent. They all started off at the beginning, so the researchers asked, how did they accomplish this?

They checked these people's work records and performance reviews and found the key strategy. When they took their first job, they would go to their boss and say, "I really want to be valuable around here. What one skill would help me the most to make the greatest contribution to this business?"

The boss would say, "Well, if you were really good at this or that, that would really increase your value. That would be really helpful to us."

So these achievers would decide on that one skill, like a sniper: one shot, one kill. They would write it down as a goal and say, "I am excellent at this skill by this date." They would make a list of everything they could think of that they could do to learn this skill—the books they could read, the courses they could take. Some of them would pay their own fees to travel across country and take courses. They would take unpaid time off if they felt it would give them an edge by studying under an expert for two days or three days. They would listen to audio programs in their car, when they were working, and when they were walking. They would watch some of the best programs on YouTube, where experts talk about their subjects.

Some people get up and watch a TED talk every morning. Now there's a whole series of TEDx that's available on YouTube as well. This is twenty minutes of time with an expert giving their best ideas on an important subject.

The achievers would focus on learning a single subject until somebody said, "You're really good at that." That would be their signal to move on to the next subject. Again, they would keep working at that until somebody told them they were good at it. These 500 CEOs all used the same strategy. They learned one key skill at a time, whether it took them a month, a year, or longer.

They would focus on that skill and read, and learn from people until they mastered it.

How many hours did they spend on this? The average person spends two hours per night, five nights a week. This was my story too. I didn't realize that research would bear it out, but when I was young and single, I never went out to bars. I'd go home and study, read, and take notes, because I love to learn.

Like everyone else, you have 168 hours in a week. Could you carve off ten of those hours to become one of the highest-paid and most successful people in your field? If you do, success is virtually guaranteed.

Albert Einstein said, "The greatest power in the universe is that of compounding." It's growing exponentially, the percentage upon the percentage upon the percentage. It's the same thing in learning. If you learn a skill and then learn another, it enables you to use the first skill even better, and probably creates more opportunities for you to use it. If you learn a third skill, it multiplies the first two skills. If you learn a fourth skill and a fifth skill, they start to multiply and compound each other. If you imagine an upside down pyramid, you start with the peak at the bottom, and as you learn, it starts to expand. Soon these people are earning ten, twenty, fifty times as much as the average person.

Anybody can do this, starting today. Anybody can say, "From now on ,I'm going to devote two hours a day to learning new skills." You can start off by listening to audio programs on your iPhone on your way to work; you can read for thirty minutes to

---

"The greatest power in the universe is that of compounding."
—Albert Einstein

---

sixty minutes each morning before you get started; you can watch YouTube videos or TED talks; you can watch documentaries or read in the evenings. Make it a ritual: you're going to spend two hours per day, five days a week, on developing that skill. That will virtually guarantee that you'll be one of the most successful people of your generation.

No Joy in Things

The final point is to realize that there is no joy in things. There is no joy in money or cars or boats. There's no joy in honors and accolades, because they're gone as soon as the applause stops and the room empties, and you're left standing there alone. There is only a fleeting joy in accomplishments.

Eighty percent of the joy in life comes from our relationships with other people. It comes from talking, living, laughing, and being part of their lives. It comes from helping your kids grow up and doing things for your spouse.

When you're with your family, be there all the time. When you're at work, work all the time you work, but when you're with your family, be there. Being there means head-to-head, knee-to-knee, face-to-face, heart-to-heart. It means that you are there, and you're in their face. You're only with another person when you're eyeball-to-eyeball with that person, not when they're down the hall, or you're in your den while they're cooking. It's only when you're face-to-face with the other person that you're truly there.

The most important thing is to ask questions, not to pontificate about what you did during the day. Ask family members about what they did and how their life is going, and then listen intently to the answers. This is the highest form of relationship: when you

---

Eighty percent of our joy in life comes from our relationships with other people.

---

take the time to listen, and to ask questions, and be patient with people. The only way to increase the value of a relationship is by investing more time in it—face-to-face time, heart-to-heart time. Turn off the television.

One study many years ago found that a child's character is formed by the conversation around the family dinner table. It's the most important single variable that determines how that young person will turn out as an adult. As a result, I've insisted that we would have a family dinner virtually every time I was home. If I wasn't there, if I was traveling, they'd have a family dinner with my wife, and they'd all talk about what they did during the day.

Never allow the television to be on during a family occasion, because people's eyes will always move to the greatest stimulus. So leave it off. If a family member comes into the room, turn the television off. If I'm working on something and someone in my family comes in, I put my reading aside and focus on them as if I'll never see them again.

Preacher Gary Smalley told this story: "Imagine that you're walking down the street, and you see coming towards you someone that you went to school with ten or twenty years ago. You haven't seen them for ten or twenty years, and you immediately remember all the things you did when you went to school. That was your dear friend. You went out on dates, and you went to parties.

"The person comes closer, and they see you. You say, 'It's you. It's you. Holy smokes.' And you hug and say, 'Gee, how are you?

A Review of Rituals for Performing at a Higher Level

- Go to bed early and get up early.
- Eat three hours prior to bedtime.
- Make a nightly list of everything you have to do the next day.
- Exercise when you get up in the morning.
- Meditate for 15-minutes every day.
- Write down six priorities each day.
- Don't check your e-mail first thing in the morning; work on priorities first.
- Eat a nutritious breakfast.
- Focus on your strengths, and delegate your weaknesses.
- Devote two hours a day to learning new skills.
- Focus on your relationships, and joy will be your byproduct.

Where have you been? What are you doing? How's your life? Are you working? Where do you live?' You have an incredibly enthusiastic conversation and maybe arrange to meet later. You walk away and think, 'Wow, wasn't that great?' You're smiling because you've seen your old friend. Then you go home and say, 'What's for dinner? Where's the TV remote?'"

Smalley's point is this: here's someone that you haven't seen for twenty years, and you might never see again in your life. You're treating them like the most important person in the world when the most important people in the world are the people at home. So when you go home and you meet a family member, look at them, and say to yourself, "It's you. Oh my, it's you." You brighten up. You smile. You're happy. You hug them. You tell them how much you love them and how happy you are to see them. I learned that when I had my first child, and I've practiced it with all my family members as well as their spouses.

If you do this one little thing, you're going to have one of the most wonderful lives you can possibly imagine. Everything else will be worthwhile.

Success in the Twenty-First Century

I have three secrets of success for the twenty-first century.

1. Your life only becomes better when *you* become better, and there's no limit to how much better you can become. The only limit is your imagination. Since your imagination is unlimited, you're going to become better and better all your life.

   One of the greatest motivations of all is the feeling of getting better. People go to a company because they feel they're going to make more progress there. People are motivated at a company because they feel they're progressing; they're learning and accomplishing new things. They will work for less money, because they're happy; they feel like winners every day. Every time you learn and apply something new, you feel like a winner. You feel happy. That's why continuous learning is so important.

2. It doesn't matter where you're coming from. All that really matters is where you're going. Almost all the unhappiness in the world today comes from people thinking and talking about things that upset them in the past. Never worry about some-

thing you can't change, and you cannot change a past event. You can only learn from the event, accept responsibility, and move on.

Leaders, the top 10 percent of men and women in our society, are intensely future-oriented. They think about the future most of the time. They think about where they're going. They think about what they want and how to get it. They think about their goals. The very act of thinking about something that you want to be or do or have makes you happy. It gives you energy, makes you more creative and personable, and releases endorphins in your brain.

3. You can learn anything you need to learn in order to achieve any goal you set. When I stumbled across this principle at the age of twenty-three, I was poor, living in a flophouse, with holes in my shoes. I had no money, no future, no education, and no experience. I came across this principle, and it changed my life forever: *I can learn anything I need to learn.*

Ever since, I've been excited about learning. The more you learn, the more you *can* learn. The more you learn, the smarter you become, because you're activating more of your neurons. They connect with others. The cells that fire together wire together. The more you fire your cells by learning new things, the more you rewire your brain to become smarter and smarter.

Usually the only thing that stands between where you are today and where you want to be is the development of a new skill. Again, all skills are learnable. You can learn whatever skill that you believe will help you double your income. Everybody who has that skill today at one time did not have it.

At this point, you're probably only one skill away from doubling your income, and now you know what it is. Write it down as a goal, make a plan, organize the plan, take the first step, and work on it every day. There's nothing that can stop you from achieving the greatness for which you were designed.

CPSIA information can be obtained
at www.ICGtesting.com
Printed in the USA
JSHW060925130423
40179JS00002B/2